THE
LAND
OF THE
DATE

THE FOLIOS ARCHIVE LIBRARY

THE
LAND
OF THE
DATE

A recent Voyage from Bombay to Basra and back, fully descriptive of the ports and peoples of the Persian Gulf and the Shat'-el-Arab, their conditions, history and customs.

1916-1917

By C. M. Cursetjee
Introduction by Robin Bidwell

Garnet
PUBLISHING

THE LAND OF THE DATE

Published by
Garnet Publishing Ltd.
8 Southern Court, South Street, Reading,
RG1 4QS, UK

This book has been re-typeset from the original 1918 edition.
For the sake of historical interest both the original page design
and original inconsistencies in the text have been retained

Copyright © 1994 Garnet Publishing

Revised edition 1996

All rights reserved
No part of this book may be reproduced in any form or by any
electronic or mechanical means, including information storage and
retrieval systems, without permission in writing from the publisher,
except by a reviewer who may quote brief passages in a review

ISBN 1 85964 038 9

British Library Cataloguing-in-Publication Data
A catalogue record for this book is available from the British Library

Jacket design by David Rose

Printed in Lebanon

CONTENTS

Introduction by Dr Robin Bidwell   vii

Foreword   ix

Original Contents   xi

The Land of the Date   1

Introduction

C. M. CURSETJEE

The Land of the Date

Cursetjee Manockjee Cursetjee, the presumed author of this book, was born in 1847, the son of a judge of the Small Causes Court in Bombay. He was sent to a nursery school run by an English lady and at the age of eleven he was taken with his brother by his father to England and left in the care of a clergyman in Southampton. In 1865 'C. M. C.', as he was generally known, went up to Christchurch, Oxford, one of the very earliest if not the first Indian to do so. The following year he was admitted to Lincoln's Inn. In 1867 he was awarded a B.A. and in June 1869 he was called to the Bar.

'C. M. C.' then returned to India where he practised in the High Court before, following in his father's footsteps, he became a judge, firstly in Ahmadnagar then in Bombay. He was one of the early members of the Indian National Congress which probably led to his being twice passed over for the Chief Judgeship of the Small Causes Court in favour of younger colleagues.

The Cursetjees were one of the leading families of the Zoroastrian community of Bombay and after his retirement from the Bench, 'C. M. C.' devoted himself to its affairs. His father had founded a school to provide Indian girls with an English education and 'C. M. C.' was responsible for making it financially secure. He was also on the governing bodies of welfare associations, hospitals etc.

At the end of 1916, at the age of nearly 70, he apparently decided that he needed a good holiday and set out on the journey that is the subject of this book. It was extremely enterprising in a man of his age to choose a war zone as his holiday destination, for Basra was the main base for the campaign in Mesopotamia which had not yet fully turned in favour of the British: General Townshend had surrendered at Kut al-Amara only six months before and Baghdad was not to be occupied for another four months. Nevertheless, as we can see from *The Land of the Date*, most of the Gulf seemed largely at peace.

It is a cheerful, charming, rather naive narrative with much of interest, providing lively pictures of the major ports on both sides of the Gulf. 'C. M. C.' enjoyed showing off his culture with quotations from Shakespeare and English and Persian poets or reflections upon history or geography. He had a very good eye for topography and his descriptions of scenery are vivid and convincing. He took an interest in everything that he saw, the technique of loading the ship, fisheries, the pearl-trade, commerce in the bazaars, architecture, food and, naturally, date cultivation, and describes them with almost boyish enthusiasm. His accounts of Bahrain before Belgrave, Kuwait just after Sheikh Mubarak and wartime Basra are full of atmosphere. His distinction ensured hospitable receptions from British officials, the Sheikh of Kuwait and leading merchants such as Kanoo of Bahrain whose way of life and business are described in detail.

Obviously the holiday did 'C. M. C.' good for he lived until he was nearly 90, dying in 1935. I am grateful to the Tata Central Archives of Bombay for his biographical details.

THE LAND OF THE DATE
OR
BOMBAY TO BUSORAH AND BACK.
1916–17.

FOREWORD.

The Start.

Many things contributed to bring about this run up and down the Persian Gulf; but it was mainly the need for thorough rest and change which I much stood in need of. It took me sometime to make up my mind for there were many good people, ready with advice—gratis,—some of whom thought it would be risky in these war days to go anywhere within 500 miles of the war zone, whilst others prophecied I should find it difficult to be allowed to get to Basra at all. I resolved however, to do it and happily met with no hurt and found no difficulty. I enjoyed an ideal holiday and saw quite a new world.

CONTENTS.

FOREWORD.

CHAPTER I.

Departure.

CHAPTER II.

The Harbour.

The lights of Bombay—View over the Apollo Bandar—Dropping the pilot—A scene full of charm.

CHAPTER III.

The Voyage out.

CHAPTER IV.

Our Ship and Captain.

CHAPTER V.

Time on Boardship.

Sights at sea—Porpoises—Flying fish—The shark—Gulls out at sea—The fish-roe—Sunrise and sunset—Sea tints—Ships that pass at sea.

CHAPTER VI.

Our Cargo and Passengers.

CHAPTER VII.
Approaching Port.

Heaving the lead—Quarantine in the Gulf—Dropping anchor—Signalling arrival—Administration of the Gulf Ports.

CHAPTER VIII.
The Madzuries.

Discharging Cargo—Interesting snap-shots.

CHAPTER IX.
Approaching Bandar Abbas.

The Gulf of Oman—Town of Jaskh—Makran—Kuh Mubarekh.

CHAPTER X.
The Gulf of Ormus.

The Salama rocks—The Island of Kishm—Death of William Baffin.

CHAPTER XI.
Visit Bandar Abbas.

The *Madzuries*—On Persian soil—Sight of the Union Jack—The Consul's resident quarters—At Dr. Burlie's house.

CHAPTER XII.
The Consulate Doctor.

His local patients—How he lives, moves and has his being.

CHAPTER XIII.

Town of Bandar Abbas.

Donkey ride—The Kuhla-i-Angrezi—The language of the country—Market by the shore—The people—Insanitary conditions.

CHAPTER XIV.

The Storm at Bandar Abbas.

Great disturbance—Sinking of a lighter—Rescue of the boatmen—*Hisab-i-khoosh ast*.

CHAPTER XV.

Account of Bandar Abbas.

Its history—Its commanding position—Water supply—Promising future—Mr. Sorabjee Dorabjee.

CHAPTER XVI.

The Island of Ormus.

Its name—Early history—Early Kings—The Portuguese at Ormus—The English at Ormus—How the East India Company squared its masters—Abandonment of Ormus—Description of the Island—Old Portuguese guns—Mineral and other products.

CHAPTER XVII.

The Persian Gulf.

The ship's course—Intermediate ports—A huge lake—Early voyageurs—Nearchus—The sway of the Portuguese—Its fall—The English in the Gulf—Pirates—Slave trading—Gun-running—Pax Britanica—Fish—Pearl-trade—Buying of pearls—The Gulf-trade—The Arab sailors.

CHAPTER XVIII.

Linga or Linjah.

Leaving Bandar Abbas—Hanjam—Town of Linga—Dr. Johnstone—The English Consul.

CHAPTER XIX.

The Bazaars about the Gulf.

The bazaar at Linga—Shops and stalls—Carpets—Mixed crowds—The Dervish—Diversity of costumes—Women in the streets—Native children.

CHAPTER XX.

Sundry Items.

The Doctor's House—The town water-supply—Kung—Shipping in harbour.

CHAPTER XXI.

Debai.

Abu Musa—Debai bay—Town of Debai—A scrap with the Chief—His truculence—His boasting—Leave Debai.

CHAPTER XXII.

The Baherein Islands.

Approaching the Islands—Heptanesia—The name Baherein—Moharek—Evening in harbour—The P. G. N. Co.'s Agent—The doctor—Missing a friend—The Sheikh—Intervention of the English—British influence—Future prospects.

XV

CHAPTER XXIII.

How we take to Land at Manamah.

How we land at Manamah—Suspended in mid-air—Sail to shore—Indifferent landing-place—The Baharein donkey—Horses—The donkey-boy.

CHAPTER XXIV.

At Manamah.

Chief town of the Islands—Houses—Flat-roofs—Narrow staircases—Badgirs—Insanitary conditions.

CHAPTER XXV.

Arab Insanitation.

The sea—beach at Manamah—Offensive sight and smells—Bad roads—Likely betterment.

CHAPTER XXVI.

Our Arab Host.

Mr. Essuf Abu Ahmed Kanoo—Coffee and coffee-pots—Coffee-drinking—Various sorts of coffee—Arab aloofness and habits—Simplicity of life—A modern Arab's office—New needs—Arab time—Tobacco smoking—Wine drinking—Coming changes.

CHAPTER XXVII.

The Baherein Bazaars.

Gardens—Garden produce—Locusts—Baherein dates—Kava-Khanas.

CHAPTER XXVIII.

Sundry Items.

Local curios—The Bohrah at Baherein—Chance for Parsees—Arab currency—The Mosque—Children at play—Boys' game.

CHAPTER XXIX.

The Baherein Water-supply.

Moharek—Sea-springs—Method of getting at them—Bir Haneini—The channel between the Islands—What might be done to improve things—The future of the Bahereins.

CHAPTER XXX.

Dejeuner à l'Arabe.

The Arab roof-terrace—View over the harbour—Arab dining-room—An Arab breakfast—Honoring the guest—Good-bye to Manamah—Return to the ship—The mounds of Ali—The Phoenicians at Baherein.

CHAPTER XXXI.

Approaching Bushire.

Kuh Khormaz—Lawless Persian tribes—Gisakan bluff—The Imambara—H. M. Man-of-War Juno—The Shah's navy—Pilots—A fine view.

CHAPTER XXXII.

Bushire.

The town—Early history—The potato in Persia—The Persian Order of Knighthood—Its origin—The Persian War—Future of Bushire.

CHAPTER XXXIII.

The City of Bushire.

The Marina—Governors—Women on the road—Persian children—Dr. Hudson's dispensary—A Parsee Captain of the I. M. S.—The Bazaars.

CHAPTER XXXIV.

The Ship's Agent at Bushire.

His office—A swell in his way—New fashion in drinks—French language in Persia—Taking aboard the *Madzuries*.

CHAPTER XXXV.

Koweyt.

Approaching Koweyt—Unreliable buoys—Fine Harbour—Early history—Phoenician settlement.

CHAPTER XXXVI.

The Town of Koweyt.

Population—Land and Water connection with Basra—Future prospects—Foiling the Turks—English influence dominant—Koweyt boats—Local gentry.

CHAPTER XXXVII.

Ashore at Koweyt.

Mr. Abdul Latif our Koweyt host—Sail to shore—Shallow waters—The breakwater—Customs house—Butchers' quarters—Koweyt honesty—The Chiefs' Courts of Justice—Boys' school—No outdoor Games.

CHAPTER XXXVIII.

We visit our Host.

The house—Up-to-date furniture—Modern Arab breakfast—Our host's hopeful—The new fashion in furniture.

CHAPTER XXXIX.

We visit H. E. The Sheikh of Koweyt.

The Sheikh's palace—His body-guard—Their appearance—The Council hall—Portrait of King George V—The Sheikh—Progress in Koweyt—The Sheikh's Motor-Car—His chauffeur—Absence of wheeled carriages.

CHAPTER XL.

The Basra Bar.

The estuary of several rivers—The Bar—Running aground—How we cross it—Dredging the bar.

CHAPTER XLI.

The Shatt'-el-Arab.

Its name—The great rivers—Mesopotamia—Land of the Five great Monarchies—In British Hands—Great possibilities—Moulana Jalal-ood-Din's reference to the three rivers—Absence of important towns on the Shatt'—Value of Kornah—Opinion of Sir John Malcolm—Life on the banks—Farms—Wild game—The buffalo—The white crow.

CHAPTER XLII.

The Land of the Date.

The word date—Cultivation of the date-palm—Flora of the Shatt country—Absence of other palms—Value of the date tree.

CHAPTER XLIII.

Date Cultivation.

The Creeks of the Shatt'—Date harvest—The beauty of the date-palm—Its many uses—Its juice not utilised—Cultivation of rice and sugar-cane.

CHAPTER XLIV.

Approaching Mohomerah.

Fao—Future of Fao—We enter the Shatt?—Abadan—Its rock-oil—Safety of oil-wells—Appearance of Abadan—Its value.

CHAPTER XLV.

Mohomerah and the Karun.

Arrival at Mohomerah—Site of town—The Karun river—The Hafar—Town of Ahwaz.

CHAPTER XLVI.

Town of Mohomerah.

Haji Mushiri—The Mirza M. Hussain—Mohomerah Bazaar—Assortment of smells—View over the Hafar—Mohomerah history—The Sheikh of Mohomerah.

CHAPTER XLVII.

Approaching Basra.

We salute the Sheikh of Mohomerah—The Sheikh's bodyguard—His palace—The barrier of sunken ships—First Sight of Basra—The weather.

CHAPTER XLVIII.

The Town of Basra.

History of Basra—Basra in the old days—Modern history of Basra—The taking of Basra by the British Indian forces.

CHAPTER XLIX.

Description of Basra.

Kinnear's opinion—A four-fold division—The Strand Road—Hack Victorias—Old town of Basra—The theatre—Bazaars—Itinerant food-vendors.

CHAPTER L.

Ashaar.

The creek—British Courts—A hamam—The American mission—Y. M. C. A.—The Venice of the East—The *bellam*.

CHAPTER LI.

The Ashaar Town.

The Basra Times—European shops—*Kava-khanas*—The High Street—Good opening for doctors—Basra climate—Cabs and victorias—An ethnological museum—The militarists in khakhi—Our new fellow-subject the Arab.

CHAPTER LII.

The River Front.

A new town on the Shatt?—War activities—Mergil—The Basraite's amazement—The Arab's expectation—Sir Arthur Lawley on the situation—Lord Hardinge's promise.

CHAPTER LIII.

British Military Rule in Basra.

Martial law—A change in the face of things—An Arab on safety cycle—Other signs of British occupation—Race-course—Prestige—The *topee*—a Britisher's views—Alcohol—Basra Times' cartoon—Reflections.

CHAPTER LIV.

A day off at Ashaar.

Parsees in Basra—The *Moodhakhal*—Beit-Vakil—The Customs house stairs—Mr. Abd-ul-Jabbar—A modern Caesar—Women in the streets—Demi-Mondaines—Wrist-watches—Our Parsee friends—Parsee Cemetry—A Parsee burial—Trip up the River—Dislocated rudder—Intrepid Arab stoker.

CHAPTER LV.

Life on the Shatt'-el-Arab.

Peasants marketing—Towing of boats—The angler and reed gatherer—Shipping on the River—Holiday-makers—Soldiers and nurses on the River—Summer visitors—Night scene—River sports of the future—Whiteman's burden.

CHAPTER LVI.

Views and Conclusions.

Law of compensation—Self—determination—British Rule in Mesopotamia—Other Arab-lands lost to Turkey—Circumstances call for a new rule—Duty of British statesmen—The 'sick man' of Europe—Deserves no consideration—Great questions—The new Government in Mesopotamia—Arab's amenability—If properly handled—Reflections—Mesopotamia possibilities—Reviving agriculture—Trade and commerce—Views on markets in China applicable—New methods to meet new conditions—The language question—Spread of Urdu—A new language—My own view—Spread and value of English—India's voice in Mesopotamia—Value of Mesopotamia to India—The bear ready to be skinned—Losing hold of Mesopotamia unthinkable.

CHAPTER LVII.

Return Voyage.

Good-bye to Basra—Zaiyanni gets aground—Great hailstorm—New Year's day—Last view of the land of the Shahs—Approach Bombay—Safely in dock.

CHAPTER I.

The Departure.

On the evening of the 7th December 1916, I stepped aboard the S. S. Zayanni, which was berthed in the Prince's dock. The ship was still taking in cargo, the blue Peter was fluttering at the masthead, and there was all the clatter and racket, of a ship's departure. There was little ceremony in passing the medical inspection; it consisting of a good hand-shake by the good-natured doctor-saheb, who pronounced me fit and smiling bid 'bon voyage!' Every body was aboard by 7 p. m. and the police took charge of the gangway, which yet kept us in touch with the shore, to prevent any unauthorised exit. Friends had come to bid good bye and had left. The pilot was aboard, the heavy gangway parted from the ship, the cables that held her to her berth were slipped, two alert little tugs took charge of the big ship, towed her clear off the wharfs, and put her in position, head first against the dock-gates. The heavy bridge, over which carriages had gone rumbling a minute before, swung round to one side, the steam-horn brayed the signal of departure, the berthing master cheerily bid us farewell and good-night through his huge extinguisher-like speaking-trumpet and the Zayanni steamed out through the dock-gate with a stately motion and took to the water in the harbor like a ship that is newly launched, just as the full moon arose clear of the misty haze that yet obscured the East. It was 9 p. m. The manœvring of a big steamer from out of the enclosed dock crowded with shipping on all sides, through the narrow water-gate is a wonderful act of scientific ingenuity and precision. The process is most interesting and must be seen to appreciate the nerve and the skill of the dock-master under whose direction it is carried out, every high tide in day-light or in the dark.

CHAPTER II.

The Harbour.

I have always felt a delight to be on the waters of our grand and beautiful harbor. This was the first time I was out on them coming out of the docks. I looked about and watched with charmed and interested eye the moving scenes. It seemed as if it was we who stood and Bombay that moved and the illusion melted away only as Bombay dropped out of sight. As we carefully picked our way out of the dock-gate, the view of the shipping on our portside, in the direction of Mazagon and Sivree, was quite faerique. The large number of ships at their moorings, many steamers but principally the heavy and ancient countrycraft, with their myriads of lights at mastheads or poop, twinkling and reflected in the waters, presented the appearance of a city of lights, silent, mystic, wonderful! Soon we passed the little rock-island with its red signal light on our starboard, and skirting it quite close, moved into the main stream, leading South to sea-ward. The sight of our 'Bombay the beautiful,' (I believe it was Dr. Waters who first so called it) as you enter the harbor in day-light is undoubtedly most striking; but 'the lights of Bombay,' present a no less striking sight as you slowly sail along from Mazagon to the Prongs well after lamp-light and when the moonlight has still not shaken off the shimmering haze. Right away from Mazagon to the Government dock-yards, is a succession of docks, wharfs, bandars, huge godowns and official buildings which compose the great and flourishing port of Bombay, multiplied scenes of our sea-borne trade activities. Here we have Bombay the busy, as much work is done all along this side of the harbour till late at night; the forest of masts looming on the sight with the crimson glow of the town lights as a back-ground and

The lights of Bombay.

the brightly illuminated tall buildings along the harbor side, make Bombay as interesting at night-time as it is beautiful by day. To the East of us, as we glided out, we had the different islands that stud the harbor, with Ooran and Karanjia and the Alibag hills, far beyond Panwel and Dharamtar. A grand panorama peaceful, yet imposing in the growing moonlight. As we passed abreast of the Yacht-club, the old Apollo bandar, Green's eating-quarter, and the amazing Tajmahal Hotel, all ablaze with light, with the lights of the new three and four storied houses that skirt the Strand Road, of the Yacht-club rookery, and the distant prospect of lofty, well-lit buildings which for a brief minute caught the eye through the lamp-lit vista of Apollo-bander Road, exposed a brilliant tout ensemble that could match any thing the most brilliant foreign city could show, astonish the incoming stranger and justly allow the Bombayite to be proud of his beautiful city,—the Sublime Porte so to say and the outer guard of all India! I kept on deck till we passed where the great Pharos on the rock-girt, storm-tossed prongs, lifts its glowing head to the skies, shedding its ray of hope and safety some forty miles to sea. It was now well passed 10.30 p. m. No 'standard time' here, but the true Sun's time that no Curzon dare standardise, or control. The pilot dropped off with a cheery 'good night'. The Kennery light to eastward still sent its distant flash as I turned in. The sea was calm and sparkled in the moon-light now clear and bright. The brineladen ozone breathed cool and fresh, giving promise of a pleasant voyage. The scene was full of charm. As we gradually lost sight of Bombay, though the glow and halo of its lights was still in view in the increasing distance, I reflected on the peace and perfect security that the mariner and the voyager now enjoys, as compared with the not very distant days, when Bombay cooped up within its moat-environed fort walls, held the wild Maharatta in dread, and the Angaria and the Sidhi played the pirates from their strongholds at Kennery and its environs.

CHAPTER III.

The Voyage.

Next morning we were well away from land, with nought but the wave below and the heavens overhead. The cold season is the best time for a voyage to Basra. The weather was perfect, cool and growing cooler as we advanced northward meeting the *Shimal*, the cold northwester of these seas. Bright sun shine by day, none too warm and beautifully bright, clear starlight by night. The sea was throughout the month of our voyage calm and unruffled. Sometimes it was like a sheet of moving glass, sometimes it gently heaved and tumbled playfully throwing up crested snowlike foam. Only twice was the evenness of the lovely weather varied by sudden storms, which however lent a striking grandeur that was in a way by no means unenjoyable. The Persian Gulf is subject to sudden but infrequent squalls, that last a couple of hours and disappear, leaving the air all the fresher and the sea lashed into fury all the pleasanter for the rare outbreak. At Bundar Abbas there was one such storm,—high winds, great peals of thunder, sparkling, vivid flashes of lightning, and heavy down-pour of rain. The other storm we experienced heralded the new year as we came in sight of Bushire after midnight; only here instead of rain, we had a grand down-pour of hail, that came clattering on the decks and beat a tattoo on the bridge above our cabin. The yearly rainfall about the Gulf, as it is called *par excellence*, is seldom much over 12 inches—the wet season prevails during the cold months. Even the most squeamish passenger, however apprehensive of *mal-de-mer*, need hardly miss enjoying the delight of such a sea-voyage as I had at this season of the year.

CHAPTER IV.

Our ship and her Captain.

Our ship the Zayanni, is a fine steamer of between 2500 to 3000 tons burden and belongs to the Persian Gulf Navigation Company of Bombay. It once belonged to the Dutch Western Nederlands Company. It is an easy, steady sea-goer, broad-keeled and perfectly amenable to her helm; even in rough weather she behaves beautifully and does her 10 knots an hour and a little more with unvarying precision. It is chiefly used for cargo-carrying and has been some years employed on the run between Bombay and Basra, touching at all the intermediate ports. Captain Kavas Ookerjee has been in command of her now for these two years. Mr. Ookerjee is in effect a *rara avis in terris*. Trained to his profession in England since he was a boy of 12, he has the rare distinction of being the only Parsee or rather the only Indian sea-captain, holding the first class Master Mariner's certificate from the British Board of Trade, having passed his several examinations with great credit. As Chief-officer and then as Captain or Master in sole command of his ship, he has served on many steamers and has made successful voyages to Europe, to the Americas, East African Coast, to Japan, to the Red sea ports, to Mauritius, and for the last several years all about the Persian Gulf of which he knows every creek, bay, island, coral-reef and harbor with an intimate thoroughness that has deservedly earned for him the high esteem of his employers of the different steamship companies he has served and is serving, whilst he is respected and admired by his ship's company for the strictness of his discipline on board, he is liked and trusted by them for his frankness and good temper, his high character and above all for his perfect nerve, his sleepless watchfulness, his high

Our Captain.

sense of duty and his skilful and expert seamanship. Many a time and oft he has sailed his ship safely into and out of the troublesome harbors of the Gulf without a pilot or with some Arab pilot, whom he has had to teach his business; and entering these harbors is no joke for they are mostly open roadsteads, shallow, treacherous with shifting sands and ill-marked rocks and reefs. Any navigation company would be proud of such an officer; but whilst the Zayanni is happy and fortunate in her Captain, I must not pass by without

<small>Our chief Engineer.</small> justly commending her chief engineer, who is a young Parsi, Mr. Shavak Driver. He too has had a part of his marine training in England. Modest and retiring, he is thoroughly well up competent and reliable at his work. He is besides a most ready and skilful mechanitian; he could turn a screw, hammar a rivet and repair marine machinery with the most capable fitter. Both our Captain and Mr. Driver were withal very good company when off duty. With them I never felt the smallest twinge of ennui during the whole voyage. They added much to the charm of it. The evenings passed enjoyably amidst pleasant talk, discussing absent friends, puzzling over the problems of the horrid German-made universal War, capping anecdotes and stories or listening to some select records on a well-toned grammophone, seated on deck, or inside, when too cold, in the Captain's snug, spacious and well-lit cabin.

CHAPTER V.

Time on Board Ship and How We Spent It.

Time on the good ship Zayanni passed most pleasantly and a bit more quickly than I wished. I could have passed another month of it with the utmost pleasure. The month I had of it was all too short. I was having an ideal time of it. It was a time of perfect rest and quiet just such as I much needed. Time did not matter except to look out for meals. Days did not count. There were no newspapers and no post, which procured a sense of peace that greatly refreshed the mind. There was never need to dress up or go into evening clothes; no callers to trouble one and no calls to make, no going out, no racket, no sports, no evening lectures, no committee meetings, such as life in Bombay is so exacting of. Promenading the ample spar decks, which the Captain and I had all to ourselves, for half an hour or so as the sun arose from the waves and again when he sank into them or after supper, when the Moon 'at length apparent queen rode in her cloudless light' and the stars who haste not, nor rest and gem the celestial vault, shone with a lustre and clearness one seldom notes or enjoys ashore. This was all the daily exercise we submitted to and even that was entirely optional. Reclining on the easy deck chairs, under the shady awning or *alfresco,* reading or not as the spirit moved one, chatting or dozing, the hours slipped past and stole away with unshod steps, calm, silent and enjoyable. The *dolcefarniente* was perfect.

<small>Sights at Sea</small>

<small>Porpoises at Sea.</small>

A cry of 'fish, fish!' and we would hurry to the ships sides to watch the wonderful spectacle of large schools of lively porpoises come alongside almost within hail and full in view, racing with the ship; members of the dolphin family, they seem full of the joy of life; rushing along emulously, leaping out and tumbling in again and churning and lashing the waves into foam and spray that seethed and whitened all around. A most interesting and exhilerating sight and one of the wonders of the deep that a land-lubber like me never wearied of watching with renewing pleasure. These hog-fish often measure eight feet, afford good oil and its flesh is by no means to be despised, so atleast say they who have to fare on it at a pinch. Just then as I saw them, and as they appeared to me in mid-ocean, with no fear of pursuit, they went gaily desporting themselves happier than boys out of school in their free life and giving no thought to the morrow. And yet what looked like fun and frolic might be panic and flight from some pursuing marine monster larger than themselves; as Shakespeare hath it:—

> 'There they fly or die like scaled
> 'Skulls before a belching whale.'

How they must have wondered at the huge bulk of the Zayanni as she ploughed through the water. Doubtless taking her for some monster leviathan, they were careful to give her a wide berth. Another wonderful denizen of the deep, which I loved to watch as part of a sea-day's pastime, is the curious flying fish, fish and fowl combined. It was most interesting to watch from over the gunwale of the high placed forecastle, a skein of these lively little fish startled by the share of the moving steamer, leap up and fly away over the water, their wet gossamer fins and wings full stretched,—

Flying Fish.

> 'Showing to the sun their waved coats dropt with gold,'

and after swift flight of some fifty yards, sink plump into the sea, vanishing from sight. In the Arabian sea one does not see so many of these pretty creatures as between Bombay and Aden. Shrimps called by the Arabs the locusts of the sea and a great variety of shell-fish abound in the Gulf of Oman and the narrow waters of the Persian Gulf. Sharks too infest them and a whale or two 'hughest of living creatures,' if not altogether myths, are occasionally sighted by the alert or imaginative mariner. But I was not in luck and never caught sight of any. The shark too is well-known in these waters and is aptly denominated '*Kalb-ol-Bahr*' or the dog of the sea. If not a toothsome victual it is said to be nutritive and 'filling at the price.' It is largely consumed by the native seafarers. Palgrave in his 'Travels in central and eastern Arabia,' mentions having had to fare commonly on shark's flesh, and how he found a dish of mutton a luxury after long knocking about the inner Gulf coasts. On the second day at sea, when we must have been well over 200 miles from any land, I was much surprised to see the sudden appearance of a pair of black-headed sea-gulls, who kept with the steamer for some hours and at sun-down disappeared. As we neared the narrowing seas of the gulf of Oman, which forms the northern end of the Arabian sea, the visits of these beautiful birds became frequent and then continuous right up to Basra. It was always a pleasant distraction to watch their graceful airy movements, untrammelled and free, now poising in mid air now skimming it, soaring above the masts or dipping to the sea, as they kept with us in the wake of the ship, their watchful eyes ever on the alert, their heads moving at will this way or that. They emitted a cheery little scream that indicated supreme content. All along the Gulf they are to be seen in gregarious flocks. Detecting a shoal of their finny prey with unerring instinct, they swoop with a whirr and settle on the sea and then follows an eager struggle with ravenous maw for the bounteous banquet. Nature kindly caters for them, doubtless to keep the ocean world from being over populated. One day when well out at sea, a pretty brown butterfly came on board, fluttered about the deck for some time and was seen no more. It was possibly born from some neglected larvae laid up in some cranny on the ship when in Bombay. Another marine phenomenon that it was interesting to observe was a curious growth which sea-men call 'fishroe'. It is sometimes seen as the ship passes through what looks like liquid rust with oily blotches on the surface that discolors the sea to some depth, quite far away from land. It is not quite clear what it consists of or whence it springs up. It is interesting and leaves one wondering. Sunrise and Sunset at sea are always glorious and the grateful eye delights to gaze on them without tiring. Getting up betimes in the morning the sight of the sea-scape towards the purpling East is entrancing, as:—

Sunrise and Sunset.

> 'Underneath Day's azure eyes...
> Lo! The Sun up springs behind,
> Broad, red, radiant, half reclined
> On the level quivering line
>   Of the waters crystaline.'

These beautiful lines of Shelley are absolutely true to nature. And again as the Sun declines along the western sky, the heavens are ablaze with a golden light, varying with tints of burnished orange, changing momentarily into hues of all the shades of jewelled crimson, opalescent, red; and as these gradually flicker and fade away, empurpling and gilding the sparkling waves and the distant horizon, there is a display of the magnificence of expiring day, such as one seldom sees or realizes on land; truly a grand conflagration on sky and sea worthy a demigod's funeral pyre, such as classic myths picture for us. Again, as on some days it was the case on this voyage, when there has been rain about, the glowing west was banked with heavy clouds, 'in thousand liveries dight,' grey, dark, silver-lined, irridescent, or gloomy and threatening. The rays of the declining sun piercing through them lent an additional grandeur to the view that arrested the eye with a never flagging wonder and charm. These seascapes would surely ravish the sight of a nature's dipsomaniac, as a lover of nature has been called.

The wonderfully varying hues and tints of the sea in sun-light and shade is another never failing source, as I found it, of enjoyment and reflection, provided you have the happy faculty of 'abstracting its enchantment.' In the tranquil passage of such a time as I was having to watch and gaze on

The tints of the Sea.

the ever changing sea-tints was a perpetual refreshment to the mind and eye. An engagement or pastime such as an artist would delight in. Truly has it been said 'they that go down to the sea in ships these behold the works of the Lord and the wonders of the deep.' By day you see the beautiful sea varying from a light green to light blue, melting into a lovely deeper blue, tinged with a faint purple towards sunset and then turn to a deep azure blue, to a quite luminous black as the dark gathers in and the stars peep out. The play of sun-light on the water is delightful. The bright emerald-green dissolving into liquid turquoise and then to a flood of sapphire or gold. As the night deepens, the good ship furrows her way through waves that gleam with a living bluish-bright flame of flashing phosphorus caused by masses of tiny fish or molluscs, with an effect that is most attractive, mystic and puzzling. The Arabs have a phantasy that this light on the sea is due to the glare of the hell-fire, an idea the ignorant Arab mind accepts without question, happy in unhesitating belief and defying argument and explanation. To them it is the will of God and that is enough. I never wearied of watching the sea with its ever present charm and change and hardly figured how time fled and winged its way. Adding much to one's lively interest and pleasure at sea, were also the many ships that passed us up or down bound for Basra or Bombay. Of 'the ships that pass at sea,' that for a moment are seen and seen no more, the most striking in these sad and strenuous days are the great white hospital-ships, with their bright green belts and large red crosses. The light of these, and we passed many of them, is most impressive in the darkness of night, distinguished from the surrounding gloom by their blazing green and red illumination. In the peacefulness the voyage procured us for the time, when we were almost forgetting it, these floating hospitals on their errand of mercy were melancholy and foreboding reminders recalling us to the sad and painful reality of the world at war. With telescope and marine glasses in hand we watched them pass, saluting them and earnestly wishing them good luck, godspeed and safety.

Ships that pass at Sea.

Whilst there was thus, as will be seen, enough to keep the voyager pleasantly occupied, banishing all ennui, life on board was all the more enjoyable and beneficial that we were entirely free from the dust and insects of sorts and pestiferous smells that our Bombay the beautiful in spite of vast expenditure of the rate-payer's money, still remains distinguished for. Dr. Johnson defines a ship as a 'prison with the chance of drowning,'—the good doctor could never have had any experience of a voyage up the Persian Gulf at this, what may be called, the beauty-season of the year in these latitudes.

CHAPTER VI.

Our Cargo and Passengers.

By the mail steamer the passage from Bombay to Basra takes seven or eight days at most. The *Zayanni* being a cargo-boat has usually to touch at seven intermediate ports, and steaming a zigzag course between the Persian and Arabian coasts, we were thus nineteen days *en route*. The boat has four three-berth cabins on the main deck and is certified to carry no more than twelve first-class passengers of whom we had very few, but we made up for this by having a large number of deck-passengers, who were left to shift for themselves as best they could about the stern-part of the ship on the cargo-encumbered lower deck. These deck passengers are a curious motley crowd, mostly Arabs and Persians, rather a rough and unkempt lot, indifferent to all personal discomfort, provided the passage-money is low. Many of them are found to prefer the open deck to the cabin, even though they could well afford to travel more comfortably. They seldom or never bathe or change clothes from start to finish whatever the distance of their destination. Our good ship was loaded up to her utmost capacity. There are four large holds, which were packed with goods with all the neatness and conveniency of sardines in a tin or herrings in a barrel, not a foot of space being allowed to be vacant, whilst the decks fore and aft were heaped with cargo carefully stacked and stowed away leaving but a narrow footway to pass up or down on either side. This war which brings hurt and loss to over half the world, procures a fine harvest in freights to the shipping companies, and the P. G. N. Co., is no way backward in profiteering by the times. The export trade to the Persian Gulf ports is made up of a variety of goods. Our cargo consisted largely of rice,

margin notes: Deck Passengers. — The cargo.

sugar, gunnies and piece-goods; whilst we had besides quantities of tea, coir-rope and house-timber ready sawn. We carried too a brand-new victoria and a lot of drawing-room furniture for an Arab employé of our ship's Agents in Basra, who expecting his goods to be carried free on the strength of his official connection, made a very wry mouth on being required and made to pay a long bill for freight.

CHAPTER VII.

Approaching a Port.

The discharging of cargo and the in-taking at the ports made a busy time of it and procured a pastime of much interest for a passenger so *désœuvré* as I was, ready for anything that was novel and worth observing. When at sea the ship's company and crew have a nice easy time of it, but in port they make up for this by much hard-work and exertion. The movement of the boat is so precisely regulated and timed under such a disciplinarian as the master of the *Zayanni*, that the arrival in port is known to the very hour. As we come to within a few miles of the port of discharge the quiet of life aboard changes to something like rush and turmoil. The Captain, who is generally his own pilot in many of these ports has to be incessantly on the bridge; the crew and the officers are at their posts. A couple of *khalasis* who heave the lead, take their stand on a sort of perch projecting from the lower deck. The lead is swung like a pendulum and heaved into the sea and pulled up every three or five minutes or so and the men sing out or drone a monotonous chant '*char balm, do fut*'!! or five or more or less as the case may be and this business has to be very carefully seen to and reckoned as the Gulf harbours are shallow and shifting. Then are the hatches lifted open, the derricks with huge chains attached are swung free, the steam-winches, two per each hatch, are ready manned and the tally-clerks and the *karani* or ship's factotum have to look alive and take their stand by the hatches, note-book in hand, whilst the necessary hands are ready inside and about the holds.

<small>Heaving the lead.</small>

Then as the port is well in view, flags spelling the ship's name are run up, the British ensign flutters at the stern, the company's flag or burgee with the letters 'P. G. N.' is up at the foremast head and beside it as was the case with us flies the ominous yellow quarantine flag, for the Zayanni was coming from a 'foul port.' At all the Gulf ports whilst plague still hangs about Bombay, quarantine regulations are more or less strictly enforced and every port has its quarantine station, most of which, situated on some remote barren island or forbidding spot secluded far from the town have a merited reputation of being regular death-traps, which help to kill, if the plague does not. Much to our amusement at the first port of call, our *karani* who is a sort of ship's manager or maid of all work, and a new hand, had described Bombay as a 'fowl' port. The intricate divergences of the English vocables were clearly beyond the karani's worrying over.

Quarantine in the Gulf.

As we near the anchorage, our Captain and pilot for the nonce all alert with eyes to the compass, and ears to the call of the lead-heaver, steering cautious and careful, shouts in stentorian tone 'station'! Straight-way the chief-officer with a *posse* of hands stands by the capstan or anchor-gear. John Chinaman, the ship's carpenter and general handy man is there too, claiming it as his proud privilege to superintend the smooth dropping or lifting of the massive anchor-chains. I found our 'John' a very amiable personage, always smiling, silent, busy.

Dropping anchor

As soon as the Captain has hit on the right spot, the order is signalled 'stop her' and the welcome word of command 'let go' is heard; at once the twain heavy anchors leaving the cat-heads, descend with a great rattling of chains and splash into the waters. The good ship is safely brought to and moored. The arrival of the ship is then signalled to the shore by a succession of terrific, ear-splitting bellowing and shrieks from the steam-horn and the siren. This latter article of the ship's furniture, useful and necessary indeed, must have been given its name on the principal of *lucus a non lucendo*. If the tuneful females, whom among other beauties Ulysses and his much battered crew encountered, had anything like the power of lungs of the

Signalling arrival.

ship's whistler named after them, those ancient mariners must have plugged their ears with wax, not from fear of being lured to destruction, as from fear of being deafened the rest of their lives.

In answer to the lovely call of our siren, the port medical officer is the first to board the ship. He examines *taliter qualiter* the ships' papers, gives a clean bill, and then and not till then is the passenger permitted to land or the cargo to begin delivery. Following the doctor, come a fleet of lighters and a boat-load of '*majuries*'. As all the Gulf ports are shallow, cargo has to be taken in or discharged in the stream, some two and half or three, sometimes even four miles away from the shore. Hence the need of the broadbeamed, cumbersome, single-masted lighters or luggers to carry goods from ship to shore and *vice-versa*. None of these ports, though much business is done there, possesses an apology even for a wharf, jetty or landing place of any sort or description. Such is the happy-go-lucky 'administration of the Gulf Ports' as it is called. If you mention this hapless state of things to the native official or even to the trader or the man-in-the-street, you are met with the invariable, 'So it is, some day make good, *Insha-allah!*' or else whatever the mischief, defect or default complained of, the usual reply is '*Ché kunam.*'! or 'what can do,' accompanied by a shrug of the shoulders, expressive of indifference or helplessness, or '*lasser-faire*' 'Why worry.'? 'Take it easy,' '*Insha-allah!*'

CHAPTER VIII.

The Majuries.

The '*Majuries*' above-mentioned, are the laborers who come aboard at every port between Bombay and Bushire, to help discharge or take in cargo. They are to look at a rowdy, vociferous body of ragged, unwashed ragamuffins, not lacking in picturesqueness. As they row or sail up crowding the flat-bottomed big boat and clamber up the ship's side, the people on board-ship call out 'here come Alibaba and the forty thieves.' An apt enough description from the look of them. Doubtless their view of *meum and tuum* is lax, and some of them might come handy as cut-throats if need be, but as a whole they are a lusty, able-bodied, lively, hard-working set of men and do the work required of them, under proper overseering, satisfactorily enough. A coarse, rough-and-tumble lot, cheery and careless, loud-toned, gutteral, stalwert chaps, fit for the job they are set to. They are mostly Arabs; the soft and sleek and more refined Mogal or Persian is not in it. With these 'forty thieves' aboard, and the equally hardy sea-men ready in the swaying lighters, the scenes on board ship as the cargo is shipped or discharged, are lively, amusing and interesting. They afford capital snap-shots. As soon as the anchors are down and the screech of the siren has called up the *majuries* the lull, leisure and somnolence usual out at sea is succeeded by feverish activity and a perfect babel of sound goes on for hours, often till midnight eight-bells, whenever a sufficiency of lighters is available, for time is of consequence. The Captain's one thought is to discharge quickly and clear away. The din, the racket and the clamour is incessant. The clatter of the winches all going atonce accompanied by the '*thad*' '*thad*' of the laboring donkey-engine, the rattle of the lumbering chains as they

Discharging Cargo.

slid in or out of the heavy iron pulleys, the hoarse shouting of the *majuries*, the boat men's sing-song chantey, the rowing and bickerings between the consignees' men and the tally-clerks, the loud cries of 'haul away', 'let go,' 'khabardar!' *'hallah'* (get on), *'maharabah'* (well done): the thumping of heavy cases that sometimes slip from the slings or bump against the ship's side, the good-natured Arab laughter, the excited complaints, bandying of jokes or abuse, all these combined to make up a remarkably assorted vociferation and a compact of sound defying description and such as the human ear seldom has the chance of enjoying or otherwise, outside a cargo-discharging in the stream in the Persian Gulf.

Whilst this went on, I found it difficult to pay attention to either book or writing-pad and so willingly marked time watching with amused curiosity the performance of the *majuries* as some of them pulled out the bags, bales or cases with eager hands or sharp hooks, and others deftly put them in the slings, by ten or twelve at a time; sometimes the pack badly roped slips when half way up and wild cries of 'look out'! 'get away,' warn the workers, who nimbly scatter and scurry like rats sighting a cat to one side or other, taking cover under the roof of the hatches to avoid the falling cargo. Such accidents seldom result in hurt or damage, owing to the watchfulness and alacrity of the men at work. At night time when work goes on, the decks in semi darkness, and the holds but dimly lighted, the sight of the roughmen, half-clad, gleaming with sweat, grabbing at the cargo, jostling one another, becomes quite weird, uncanny and dantesque. With these *majuries* the work being well pushed on as it was on the Zayanni under the constant pressure of the Captain who has to act as his own stevedor, 5000 bales on an average could be slung over-board in a matter of twelve hours or less. Beyond Bushire, at the other Gulf Ports and up the Shut-el-Arab no local *majuries* are to be found, so that the steamers going further up have to ship a sufficient company of these useful 'forty thieves' at Bushire for the rest of the journey to Basra and back to Bushire. The men thus earn their wages, get their food and enjoy in the bargain a pleasant voyage,—except of course during the torrid hot months, when labor is real hardship and life becomes nigh to unbearable and the engaging of sufficient hands becomes a serious trouble to the cargo-boats, and the consignees.

CHAPTER IX.

Approaching Bandar Abbas.

Bandar Abbas the port so named after Shah Abbas the Great, is the first Gulf-Port we made, outward bound. The Arabian Sea, which bounds the western coast of India northwards from Bombay, is broadest between Maskat and Karachi in a straight line, West to East. I regretted much the Zayanni did not touch at either of these places, as sometimes it does. Better luck next time perhaps—*Insha-allah*! The northern end of this sea forms the narrowing Gulf of Oman—so named from the long stretch of the south-eastern coast of Arabia ruled over by the Imaum of Maskat. Passing Cape Jaskh, the Gulf of Oman becomes so narrow that the sea-farer comes within sight of land on both sides all day long. We are here as we proceed onward between the land of the ancient Elamites on our right and on our left the land of the Ishmaelites. The latter coast stretching northwards forms the huge promontory of Oman, fitly called *Ra&s-el-Jabel* or Cape of mountains, where not far inland stand like sentinels in a line the high and bare peaks of Mt Kava rising nearly 6000 ft; Mt Harim 7000 ft; Mt Fine 4500 ft and Mt Sibi 3000 ft. high. These solitary peaks are seen keeping ward and watch over 'the vasty wilds of wide Arabia'. This great promontory divides the Gulf of Oman and the Persian Gulf, its eastern side barren and mountainous, whilst much of the west of it is flat and fertile.

<small>The Gulf of Oman.</small>

The little town of Jaskh, situated on the south-western end of the Mekran coast, someway inland from Cape Jaskh, is a Persian fishing village, easily seen from our steamer as it stands on the sandy shore backed by and as it seemed surrounded by interminable ranges of low barren hills. Very

<small>The Town of Jaskh.</small>

early in the 17th century there was an English trading factory established here, which was the object of attack by the Portuguese raiders. Accordingly there were fought two sea-fights off this town. The first was indecisive, but in the second encounter in 1620 'the Portugals' were signally worsted by the East-India Company's ships and their claim to undisputed 'freedom of the sea' in these Indian waters, because Vasco Da Gama was the first to round the Cape, met with defeat. It was the first stunning blow their power met with at the hands of their rivals in the East from 'the right little tight little Island' over the seas. The taking of Ormus later completed their downfall in these latitudes, as it dealt a crushing blow from which they never recovered. Jaskh has now risen into some importance owing to its being the Anglo-Persian Telegraph Co.'s station, whence the submarine telegraph cable runs on one side to Maskat, on the other to Karachi and again up the Gulf to Bushire, Fao and Basra, going thence further north and away to the Mediterranean. It has a British Vice-Consul, and a Doctor, who with a small staff of the Telegraph Co., must be having anything but a happy time of it in this solitary spot. They deserve our pity as well as our admiration, for it can only be their zeal and indomitable devotion to duty under the British flag, which floats free over the Consulate, that could reconcile them to where their lines are cast in anything but pleasant places. One could well imagine their feeling must be like that of men marooned and cut off from the civilised world.

I may note here *en passant* that the name 'Makran' given to this wild hilly province of south eastern Persia has a curious derivation. It is said to be composed of the Persian words *Mahi & Khuran*, meaning fish-eaters. I am however, doubtful of this too facile interpretation. The dwellers of the entire Gulf litoral and of the Oman shores largely live on fish and so one would think all these extensive countries would be called 'Makran'. Sir P. Sykes imagines the name as coming from *Maka and Aranya* that is to say, the wastes or swamps of Maka, the latter word being supposed to have been the early name of this country. *Aranya*

Makran, derivation of.

is given as the Sanscrit for a marsh, or jungle and is equivalent to or reminiscent of the word '*ran*' as found in the terms Ran of Kutch and Matharan. 'Who shall decide where doctors disagree'? I shall tide over the point as my munshi used to do when faced with a poser, 'Khair lets get on with the next.'

Kuh Mubarakh.

Just turning Cape Jaskh, you come in sight of a remarkable hill or dark precipitous rock called *Kuh Mubarakh*, some 330 feet high. Like a huge round tower it rises sheer out of the sea, detached a short way from the Persian shore, a prominent land-mark for the coasting country craft. So evidently named by the native mariners the *Kuh Mubarakh* or the happy hill or the hill of hope, in gratitude for perils past in these treacherous seas. On the southern side high up of this hill-tower there is a curious perforation cutting right through and visible if caught at the right angle, in clear weather. This rock might some day be easily turned into a second Hell-goland, as an impregnable outer-guard, a far-sighted sentinel on the Persian Gulf. It would be well if the Union Jack were hoisted on its summit in good time, before the intriguing German octopus' unscrupulous, insidious and avid tentacles get at it.

CHAPTER X.

The Gulf of Ormus.

Early in the morning of the 12th December, the fifth day after leaving Bombay we entered the straits of Ormus, which sweep out from the north end of the Gulf of Oman, into the Persian Gulf westward, rounding the far-extending promontory or peninsula of Oman with its great cluster of rocky islands and coral shoals. On our right extends the Persian Coast of the extensive district very truly and aptly called 'Biaban' or the desert, for it shows nothing, as far as eye could stretch, but bare, jagged, mountain-peaks and sterile narrow valleys between, without any trace of water, or sign of life. Not even a kite or eagle, 'the native burghers of sequestered hills,' was to be seen anywhere here. A little further up, we here passed the extremely craggy *Ras* (head-land) *el Mus-sendam* (the anvil), appropriately so called because of the heavy, surf-laden seas that unceasing dash and strike sledge-hammar-wise against and all around it. It forms the extremity of the northern promontory of Oman, a vast wilderness of low, uneven, rocky peaks of basalt or granite, and called the *Ras-el-Jibbal,* already above mentioned. Here we entered the straits of Ormus, coming abreast of a remarkable group of three rocks or rocky islands, happily or by way of securing good augury, called *the Salamas,* safety or salutation. This is evidently an euphemism, these singular rocks being so named by the early Arab mariners to propitiate the evil spirits who, they believed, haunted them and caused constant ship-wrecks on their dangerous shallows. These rocks are also known as the great and the lesser Quoigns. A lofty ridge which is close to and screens off the city of Mashad from the eyes of the pilgrims coming from Teheran and the Western parts of

<small>The Salama rocks.</small>

Persia to visit the sacred tomb and sanctuary, is also similarly called 'kuh-Salama'. The passage between them and Cape Mussendam is called *El bab* or the Gate and is the true gate-way into the Persian Gulf. They stand as sentinels to greet and welcome friends and guard against hostile intruders. These three outstanding island-rocks or masses of basalt, which reminded me somewhat of the Needles off the Isle of Wight, are also called Arab-fashion the '*Benat-es-Salamah*' or 'the daughters of safety'—and they may now be taken to justify somewhat this poetic appellation because of a conspicuous and very necessary light-house on the largest of these rocks, maintained I believe by the British or Indian government. When I passed by them, as the Zayanni steered her way cautiously onwards towards Bandar Abbas, which here came into full view, the Salamas a mass of burnished gray under the forenoon sun looked tranquil and beautiful in spite of their bare and inhospitable shores where not even a bird was to be seen; the liquid turquoise-like sea tremulous with silver sheen, running in between these rocks, and breaking on their sides with lovely, foam-tipped, rippling wavelets, bestirred by a gentle breeze. Except the resident light-house keeper and his staff, whose lot, though they seemed to be comfortably housed, I do not envy, there was no other sign of life, not a tree to give shade, not a vestige of verdure to refresh the eye. As we advanced, we had the small 'dreary looking, rock-girt' island of Lerak on our right and a little further up on our left the large island of Kishm or Djishim. The latter is also called '*Jazirat-i-diraz*' or the long island and is the largest in the Gulf. There is

<small>The island of Crshm.</small>

a small village of the same name on its extreme north-eastern outjutting point. A long, narrow and intricate sea-way between this island and the mainland gives ships of small burden a shorter passage to Lingah from Bandar Abbas, but for larger vessels the outerway to the south side is always preferred as the safest. The cautious skipper follows the Persian proverb '*rast ro garche dur ast*'—or go by the right road though it is a long one. The Kishm village has an interesting connection with English maritime history, which deserves recalling. At the time when the East India Company joined forces with Shah Abbas against the Portuguese in Ormus, a small naval party was landed here, attacked and took the village, and one of the only two Englishmen who were killed in the fight, was the celebrated navigator William Baffin, the adventurous discoverer of Baffin's Bay. A number of fishing smacks, some Arab *buggalows* with single mast and hugh canvass were seen lazily hugging the shores and our friends the graceful sea-gulls in larger crowds helped to enliven the scene. Steaming further northward, now well within sight of the port of Shah Abbas the Great, we slowly passed about four miles on our star-board the famous Island of Ormus, and soon after close upon noon we cast anchor in the first harbor I made in the Persian Gulf.

CHAPTER XI.

Visit to Bandar Abbas.

From our deck the town of Bandar Abbas looked beautiful and inviting. It was clearly a case of 'tis-distance lends enchantment to the view'. With its clustering flat-roofed whitened houses, its long sea-beach and a back ground of distant hills, among which towers sky-high the peak of Jib-el-Bakhun, rising over 10,500 feet, it made a pretty picture. The British Consulate doctor, Dr. Burlie, was the first to step aboard and greet us in a very friendly fashion. In his wake I caught my first sight of the *Majuries* or 'Alibaba and the forty thieves,' as they are facetiously called; a heavy boat-load of them coming along to clear the cargo. They crowded every square inch of a large, heavy shore-boat so common in the Gulf. They made a picture that took my mind back to the days when Sinbad the Sailor sailed these seas. The make of their boat, the fashion of their clothes, their figures and appearance all seem hardly to have changed. The boatmen rowed in a fashion that is peculiar to them; seated right on the gunwales on either side and facing each other athwart the width of the boat. A loud voice sang out a sort of cantique to the rhythm of the oars, as these leisurely dipped and feathered, and the whole body of *Majuries* responded with a raucous refrain. These boat-songs are often a source of great merriment to these sailor-men, as they are full of impromptu topical hits and satirical allusions to the passengers, as well as to their townsmen. Capt. Ookerjee is on very good terms with most of the British officials who man the Gulf on both its shores, so that being obliged to remain on board to look after the discharging of cargo, of which the boat had over 5000 packages to clear out here, he put me and our chief engineer in

[margin: The Majuries at Bandar Abbas.]

charge of Dr. Burlie, who very kindly took us ashore in his gig or boat manned by half-a-dozen sturdy Arab oars-men. The distance between ship and shore was (if I misjudge not) something under four miles. With a feeling of eager curiosity to see the first Persian town in my experience, early in the afternoon we set foot on the soil of Iran, the ancient homeland of the Parsees. For the first time on the classic and storied ground of Persia, in the land of Jamshed and Kaikhoosroo, of Rustam and Afrasiab, of Hafiz and Firdausi, I felt quite elated and the more so and greatly interested too was I, to remember that it was on this very spot that I trod on and in its immediate vicinity the old Iranian ancestors of the Parsees had halted and made their abode when fleeing from the tyranny of their Arab masters, as well as from the over zealous persecution of their erst-while co-religionists perverted to Islam. It was hence, that the wave of persecution driving them out, they set sail and made for the hospitable shores of tolerant India in successive ship-loads. I could not help picturing these Parsee pilgrim-fathers adventuring on to them the unknown seas, (which I had just crossed over so comfortably) in the fragile and primitive vessels such as are still used in these places, making a voyage then so fraught with perils by sea and land. The Bandar, as it is yclept by way of distinction, like all Persian ports, does not, in fact just declines to, boast of a pier or landing- place whatever and as the sandy and muddy strand is shallow, even the Doctor's rowing boat had to stand out some twenty yards away from it, and we had to get to it on the backs of the boat-men who waded thigh-deep in the waters. The Doctor's house and the British Consulate with its clustering residences for the Consul's staff, stand a good way off the town, on the east side of it nearly facing the Island of Ormus. We had no time to go and pay our respects to the representative of British power, much as I wished to have done; I looked however with pride at the Union Jack, the 'glorious rag of England,' the 'flag that's braved a thousand years' of successive fights crowned with victory for civil liberty and in the best interest of Law and ordered civilization, over more than half

On Persian Soil.

Sight of the Union Jack.

The Consul's House. the habitable globe. India is loyal to the flag for all it represents and I reverently saluted it. Built of fine dark stone, quarried in the Isle of Ormus, the Consul's house here is the finest to be seen anywhere on the Gulf litoral. It is an upper-storied building, with spacious verandahs and a balustraded flat roof such as is common everywhere hereabouts. It is surrounded by an extensive compound in which stand other buildings and out-houses for the consulate establishment. The doctor's house is close by, with its low-walled compound, very comfortable, with many rooms and airy corridors to keep it cool.

At Dr. Burlie's House. To get to it we had to wade through a long stretch of desolate sandy waste, making anything but pleasant footing. Roads there are none, even of the most primitive sort, anywhere in all the towns and cities on the Gulf. Dr. and Mrs. Burlie gave us a very friendly reception. We spent an hour with them, taking tea and looking over a large collection of excellent photographs of views and people taken by the Doctor, who is an enthusiastic and capable amateur with the camera.

CHAPTER XII.

The Consulate Doctor.

Wherever there is a British Consulate hereabouts, there too is to be found a good capable doctor, drafted from the Indian Medical Department, with a well-supplied free dispensary, which is certainly one of the causes that make the British popular with the people everywhere in the Gulf. The dispensary is 'a boon and a blessing' and is largely resorted to by the poor, most of whom suffer much from eye and stomach troubles, brought on by the all-prevailing sand, flies and insects, the unhealthy water supply and habits that show that anything like ablution and personal cleanliness are reckoned superfluous in Persian life and living. The better classes too, readily avail themselves of the skilled services of the *Ingrezitabib-sahib*, only they generally prefer to fee him by results, which does not add much to the doctor's official income. The Persian gentleman's or lady's idea seems to be that if you get well it is the hand of God and so *Sukhr Allah!* thanks be to God. If you don't improve it is the fault of the Doctor—then why pay? Dr. Burlie amused us much by many stories of how his better-class patients tried to evade payment till in all such cases he properly insists on payment in advance and rightly retaliates on his close-fisted patients with, 'if you get well the credit is the doctor's; if you don't, it's *Kismet!*' This appears to be the case everywhere in this ancient-land with the English doctor and his native clients. Sometimes the Arab as well as the Persian try to square or do the doctor with the giving of a carpet or a foot-rug more or less worthless, or a trayful of indigestible sweets or a brass-pot or potsherd said to be antiques. So that the system of cash first and physic afterwards, is clearly the correct process with these by-no-means-unsophisticated gentry of the

Gulf. If the laborer is worthy of his hire, surely the doctor in the Gulf ports stands pre-eminently so. For many months together he has a hard and unenjoyable time of it surely, in these desolate places where his lines are cast, unless he is keen on archaeology or semetic languages or indulges in some similar all-absorbing fad or pursuit to occupy his leisure; sport is there if he is a decent shot, but it is expensive and involves much trouble and exertion. Decent and desirable society there is next to none. If unmarried his leisure is aggravated by solitude unless he hobnobs with the native. If married, his life is one of anxiety if his family is with him, and if not, then one of expense as he is bound to keep two establishments. Of course where there is the consulate or residency, there is always a club, with its more or less forlorn gymkhana grounds, where the few meet to make company over tea and tittle-tattle, and a library of ill-stocked contents where one can regale on well-thumbed ancient literature with all its dullness of twice-told tales, or revel in newspapers a fortnight old, which too, in these war-days with postal dislocation, come in fit-fully and ill-assorted. The good doctor of these ports is hard hit too by the world-worrying War. His salary by no means munificent is paid in rupees, and as the currency all over Persia is regulated by the Persian '*kran*' which in exchange value just now is very high and keeps rising, the doctor's income necessarily suffers increasing reduction. Under all these circumstances these doctors leading as they do a life of professional devotion and self-sacrifice deserve our cordial admiration and sympathy.

CHAPTER XIII.

Visit to the town of Bandar Abbas.

Bidding good bye to Dr. and Mrs. Burlie, 'the chief' and I proceeded to inspect the town of Bandar Abbas. As there was no road to speak of and a good way to go ankle-deep in loose sand which owing to a damaged leg I was unequal to, the doctor kindly procured me a Persian client's riding donkey. Of fine breed, coal-black, silken-skin, ambling-paced and gaily caparisoned with embroidered *Khorgin* or saddle-bags and a soft cushion of well-cured leather for saddle he made a comfortable mount. Astride him, legs dangling as there were no stirrups, a donkey-boy steering him held by the head, and my friend the amiable young 'chief,' footing it along-side, long staff in hand, we readily made a picture that you would find in any illustrated Aesop's Fables of the old man and his son taking their ass to market. Walking and stumbling we reached the town and entered and passed through many devious, crooked lanes with blank white-washed walls, through which only an aboriginy could find his way. Wishing to see the bazaar we went straight to it, but finding it so dark and dirty and so redolent with smells such as our unaccustomed nostrils were ill able to stand, that we cleared out of it double quick and got out on to the open strand in front of the town and went on along this to visit, what our guide described as an object of travellers' curiosity, called the '*Kulah-i-Ingrezi*' or the Englishman's hat. It is a large, high, red-colored, much dilapidated building at the western end of the busy bazaar, with a tall cupola curiously shaped like a brimless pot-hat. Nobody could inform us what it originally was intended for. Possibly it is the remains of a factory the English or Dutch had formerly

Donkey Ride.

The Kulah-i-Ingrezi.

established in this place. There was once an English factory here, which was destroyed by the French about 1759 and had to be abandoned. It is evidently old for it is very dilapidated and is now used as a sort of Customs' warehouse for the goods that are landed on a sort of rough jetty close by. The entrance was crowded by coolies going in and out carrying loads, and the interior looked so dark and noisome that we cared not to enter it. Dismissing the donkey, the Chief and I took a leisurely stroll along the sandy beach. Here were drawn up a large number of boats, some noisily putting off or unloading goods, others, keels upwards, were being calked and careened, amidst a crowd of sailors and seamen of sorts, jabbering, quarrelling, shouting, busy, or pretending to be; mostly idling, lolling about or lounging, seated on their hams or standing, producing a miscellaneous volume of sounds which even the most erudite of Arabic scholars like Niebuhr or Palgrave or Palmer would be at a loss to make much of. It is such a confused jumble of the patois and provincialisms prevailing along all parts of the Gulf coasts, with Afghan, Persian, Hindostani and Beloochi words and expressions thrown in, as to fully justify its being popularly called 'lisan-at-taiyoor' or the language of birds, to understand which you must be brought up in it or have a special gift. Troops of children, girls and boys, small and big were seen playing, prattling, racing, fighting, screaming, crying and laughing. Here too is the daily fish-market, where buyers and sellers were having a high-time of it, chaffering, questioning, gesticulating, asserting, denying amidst heaps of fish fresh, stale, dried, raw or fried, crammed in baskets or laid out on dirty cloths or on the bare sand or strung up on poles. Extemporized cook-stalls were also to be seen, cooking kabobs or scraps of meat, doing a thriving trade surrounded by crowds of struggling and screaming purchasers. A busy and interesting scene. The men, mostly Persians in their blue-calico *Jama* or frock-like dress, baggy trousers flowing or tied at the ankles, tattered white cotton *papoush* down at heels on feet and ugly ball-shaped felt hats;

The Sandy Beach at Bandar Abbas.

Arabs too were there, numbers of them, with their distinctive colored or plain white *kafiyeh* or kerchiefs held on their heads with camelhair bands or merely by common white cords, long inner coat with rough woolen brown or black over-alls, and more or less ornamental sandals, on feet. Here too were innumerable, pranksome little folks with hardly any clothes on at all, ragged guttur-snipes and gamins, barefooted, bareheaded, dirty, but free, careless debonair and indifferent to all but the fun and need of the present hour. Women were not to be seen about excepting just a few of the lower classes, looking like moving mummies or bales of black-cloth, covered from head to foot, not a vestige of form or feature to meet the curious eye. A few ugly-looking mangy dogs and some ownerless donkeys formed part of the general company and added to the general clamor and variety. Amused and interested, we should have liked to have lingered watching the much-varying scene so full of life and color, but we had to beat a hastly retreat. Underneath a lovely, clear sky, with the beautiful blue waters rippling ashore, the entire beach recked with horrid stench and smells that assailed our lungs and nostrils and were of so composite and so penetrating a character as to defy defining. Offal and refuse of every variety, putrid fish and leavings of the cook-shops, burning tow and tar, rotting vegetables, verminiferous rags, dead animals, asses' dung strewed the whole length of the strand which if these Persians cared for it could be made into so fine a public promenade, ... whilst *horescoreferens* grown-up men and children sat close to the water's edge paying nature's calls, regardless of decency or privacy, with only the tide for their toilet and flushing-system combined. We really had to run for it and that again was no joke for the sand was heavy, or wet and soft close to the sea and the entire beach was scattered with loose shingle and shells, broken-up cargo-cases, discarded boats-gear, rotting masts, disused old anchors, scraps of all sorts, rusty nails and hoop-iron, whilst there were boat-cables stretched across from the prows to beyond high water-line; all this as may be imagined made movement slow and precarious. We however struggled through and got carried aboard the Doctor's boat, which he kindly had placed at our disposal and so ending our visit to Bandar Abbas, we gained the Zayanni without scathe or damage to health or limb.

CHAPTER XIV.

The storm at Bandar Abbas.

And it was just as well we made our hurried departure, for had we lingered ashore another hour or so, we should have been caught in a tremendous storm, such an one as are usual in the Gulf, that burst over the harbour, in which in a small open boat with three or four miles to make in a raging sea, we should have found ourselves in a tightish predicament. Early in the afternoon I had noticed clouds gathering about the hills of Ormus, and the sudden stillness of the air, and intermittent lightning flashes in the South betokened the coming storm. Luckily we got 'home' to our steamer in good time just after the sun went down amidst masses of angry, lowering clouds, fronting a chequered crimson sky. The cargo-discharging was just about finishing when loud roars of thunder heralded the coming of the tempest. The hatches were sharply closed down, tarpaulins stretched over the deck-cargo and things hurriedly made all taut and ship-shape, when down came a deluge of rain, in a heavy incessant pour, with loud and rapid thunder-claps, quick-blazing, rattling flashes of lightning, and furious squalls of wind blowing from every quarter of the heavens. Darkness came down like a black pall or curtain hiding every thing from sight. The sea so placid only an hour before—rose in huge yesty waves that dashed against and over the ship's sides, seething with fury. Here was heard 'the mighty voice of the sea' with thunder mingled.

> The 'Outrageous Sea, dark, wasteful wild,
> Up from the bottom turned by furious winds
> And surging waves, as mountains to the assault.'

It was a magnificent sight this grand play and display of nature's power. It doubtless did some damage, but rain was much wanted all along this coast. This is the rainy season in the Gulf. There was some rain the day before, but not sufficient, and people were anxiously watching for more. The town's and country's water supply depends largely on these sudden rain-storms, which may thus be taken gratefully as providential and beneficent. We were happy or hapful that this grand atmospheric disturbance overtook us whilst still safely at anchor and not when just shortly after we had to thread our way through the strait and rock-strewn passage out between Bandar Abbas and our next port of Lingah. To judge of the fury of the storm it may be mentioned that just as the full lighters had safely cast off and were making all sail to shoreward, a belated boat, with some ninety bags of sugar which had to be transshipped, endeavored to come along-side, when an immense sea rushed and swamped it. Down went the lighter to the bottom; the four or five men in charge of it were seen struggling for life in the seething and raging waters, and but for the humane exertions of our Captain would have been food for the fishes. Under his urgent orders, the drowning men were rescued and hauled up on deck. There was no means of putting them ashore that night, so they were carried on to Lingah, whence they must have got to their homes in a day or two by some coasting smack, much to the astonishment, delight or may be the disappointment of their families, who must have given them up for lost to a certainty. For the moment the fortunate boatmen, who so narrowly escaped a watery grave, must have felt that their '*hisab-i-khoosh-ast*,' or their account correct, a common Persian exclaimation when anything dangerous or critical unexpectedly turns out satisfactory.

CHAPTER XV.

Account of Bandar Abbas.

The town of Bandar Abbas is situated on the north side of the straits of Ormus and is the seaport of the province of Kirman or Caramania. It has a population of about 12000 to 15000, a good portion of which consisting of Bagdadis, Arabs, Armenians, Afghans, Baluchis and Scindhis may be considered to be of a floating character. It stands on the site of what was once the town of Gombrun, the Cambaroa of the early Portuguese writers, now little heard of or remembered so completely has the name disappeared since the great Shah Abbas made the place his principal sea-port and named it after himself. It frequently changed hands between the Sultans of Maskat and the Persians. Eventually the former was expelled in 1868 and the latter took final possession of the place and appertaining districts and installed a Persian governor there. Besides the British, there is now the Russian and Belgian Consulates there and the B. I. and the P. G. N. Co.'s steamers call there regularly. Its commanding position at the entrance of the Gulf and being the starting point of four great trade or caravan routes into the interior, would in better hands, turn its present insignificance into one of great commercial importance. At a distance its array of white-fronted houses bathed in sunshine, give it a very pleasing appearance, but at close quarters it is a disappointing, ill-built, dilapidated place, surrounded by a desolate plain with hardly a tree to be seen, and backed by the frowning range of the bare and bleak Shamil mountains in the distance. The houses are mostly tumbled down, single-storied, flat-roofed, with not a minar nor minaret to relieve the ugliness and monotony. It is considered extremely unhealthy, and there can be no doubt of this

Its History.

owing to the prevailing uncleanliness one sees at every step and turn. The health-officer or the scavenger are here clearly unknown and any idea of hygiene or sanitation has evidently no room in the Bandar Abbasi's head-piece. The town's water supply is procured from some cisterns built far towards the East of it, and has to be fetched in jars or water-skins that never seem to be cleansed, carried on backs of donkeys or on the shoulders or heads of poor women. Such as it is what passes for drinking water is scanty and at best could hardly be said to be potable. The few English residents manage through the courtesy of the Captains to get their supply of Bombay water from the storage of steamers visiting the place. The generality of town people I fancy seldom have a regular bath such as we understand it outside the land of the Shahs and Caliphs, whilst the sea-faring populace usually have such involuntary wash as their calling necessarily provides. With a more intelligent and honester Government, with better roads, a railway at all events as far as Bushire along the coast, proper sanitation, a water supply from the neighbouring mountain-sides and tree planting could I am sure, turn this present lifeless, rotten town into a stirring and flourishing city. So long however, as the place is cursed with such Government as it has and the people, sluggish and apathetic, are content with their miserable lot, with their eternal '*che qunam?*', there is small chance of improving the port of Shah Abbas and the possibilities that are there are little likely to be realised. The same may be said of the whole country, which badly wants fertilising, stirring and waking up. When I was there there was a certain amount of stir and activity, as a new telegraph line was being run over the mountains, and men and animals at work were in evidence and much material in the shape of reels of wire and timber-posts etc. was being collected to be transported into the interior.

    I regretted much the shortness of my stay prevented my visiting Mr. Sorabjee Dorabjee, who is established in this place for many years now and is carrying on considerable business as a merchant and contractor in a large way.

Mr. Sorabjee Dorabjee.

He started with the usual modest 'Europe shop' and is now held in much consideration as a *Malek-at-Tujar* or prince of merchants. With the native patience, perseverance, prescience and energy which distinguishes a Parsee thrown on his own resources, Mr. Sorabjee has greatly flourished. Besides his local dealings among which he has I am told, just then on hand a contract of over two lacs of rupees to supply camels to the British military authorities; he does large business with Bombay and elsewhere in the red ochre called *Gilek*, of which there are extensive deposits, rock-salt and minerals such as are found in considerable quantities on the Island of Ormus. He has a large house in the town facing the sea, with a shop and godown on the ground floor. It stands next door to what was pointed out to me as the Governor's palace. Both these structures had a very shaky and dilapidated look, peculiarly Persian.

CHAPTER XVI.

The Island of Ormus or Hormuzd.

Approaching Bandar Abbas, as we enter the harbour, on our right uprises from the sea, the island of Ormus or Hormuzd famous once for its fabulous riches, 'the wealth of Ormus and of Ind' as sung by Milton. It faces the mouth of the river Minab, which flows into the sea to the East of Bandar Abbas. It is divided from the shore by a narrow channel of about four miles width. The name is derived either from Hormazd, worshipped by the ancient Persians, the powerful opponent and eventual conqueror of Ahriman the spirit of evil, or more likely as some contend it was Khormaz from *Khurma*, the Persian for date, as the surrounding country further inland is known as *Moghistan*, meaning the land of date-palms and the early accounts record that the place was celebrated once for the excellence and abundance of its dates. It is evidently the '*Armonza Polis*' mentioned by Ptolemy. The Island, formerly called *Jerun*, must have in very early times formed part of the mainland to the north of it, where once stood further inland the ancient town of Hormazd and where it was, no doubt, that the ancient followers of Zarthust, wandering away out of Fars, Kerman and Khorasan settled and abode for many years. No trace now remains of the old town except extensive ruins. The Island must have then formed the chief port of this part of Persia and became renowned from as far back as the 13th century as the chief emporium of trade between India and all Asia and Europe through Syria and Asia Minor. In 1442 an envoy of Shah Rukh, King of Persia, on his way to one of the courts in India, visited the Island and describes it as 'the vast Emporium of the world,' frequented by merchants from all parts of Asia and Arabia, dealing in every

Its name.

description and variety of silks, metals, gold, gems, pearls, arms and weapons, brocades, valuable cotton goods, spices, curious birds, and wild animals. Hence the renown of the fabulous wealth of Ormus. As was the case in early times with the greater part of the southern coast-lands of Persia, the Island with its wealthy hinterland was originally ruled for a long course of years by Arab chiefs and kings, who came across the Gulf from Oman and other parts of central Arabia and founded their petty dynasties, till the Arab King of Hormasd, driven by the ever recurring Tartar inroads, removed to the Island itself. Somewhere about the 1507, when the Portuguese power spreading northwards from Goa made incursions in and formed strongly fortified settlements all over the Gulf, the King of Ormus was over-powered by the memorable Portuguese Viceroy, Alphonsa D'Albuquerque, and became tributary to Portugal and the place remained subject to that far away European country for nearly a century. Though nominally under its Arab king the Portuguese really held sway. With Ormus in their firm grasp, they made settlements in other parts guarded by strong forts and so commanded the seas within and without the Persian Gulf. From time to time they went through the form and ceremony of electing the King of Ormus. This is mentioned by an early Italian traveller, who writes, 'when the old king died, the Captain of the Portugals chooseth another ... and sweareth him to be true to King of Portugal ... He is honored as a King, but he cannot ride abroad without the consent of the Captain first had.' Later came 'John Company, Bahadoor' on the scene and ousted the 'Portugals' as Pepys, the delightful diarist, calls them. Shah Abbas, the most capable and remarkable of the later Kings of Persia, who had long cast a longing and envious eye on Ormus and was jealous of the Portuguese power and much irritated by their growing arrogance, now stepped in and with the ready help of the English ships and soldiers, besieged the Island, which after a protracted and gallant defence,

Its early Kings.

The Portuguese at Ormus.

The English with Shah Abbas at Ormus.

surrendered and so passed into the hands of the Persians. The service the English rendered to the great Shah was not without ample return from the booty they insisted on sharing at Ormus and from various important concessions obtained from the Shah, besides triumphing over their Goan rivals.

<small>The E. I. Co's booty and what they had to pay for it.</small>

But the Company had to pay pretty heavily to salve the conscience of their masters, the good King Charles and his prime favorite the Duke of Buckingham, who questioned the Company's authority to levy arms against a friendly power; for though there was chronic warfare between Goa and Bombay for supremacy at land and sea, just then Portugal was under the crown of Spain, between which power and England there was peace. Accordingly, as the record of those transactions nicely phrases it, both the minister and his royal master *'had to be sweetened,'*—a very pretty and expressive phrase and so out of the captured spoils and treasures of Ormus, the Company wisely paid a *douceur* of £10,000 to each of them. The taking of Ormus dealt a staggering blow to the power of the too presumptuous Portugals, and opened the free navigation of the Gulf to the English. The Island of Ormus being thus wrested from the Portuguese, Shah Abbas removed all his establishments from it to the neighbouring town of *Gombrun*, which then became Bandar Abbas!

<small>Abandonment of Ormus.</small>

<small>Description of the Island.</small>

The island town of Ormus thereafter dwindled in importance and value and is now become a mere hamlet with hardly a population of a thousand souls. This once famous Island, the meeting house of nations—is some sixteen miles in circumference and about four and half miles across. As seen from the ship it offers to view confused masses of reddish brown hills, rising sheer from the sea, without any landing-place visible. The peaks and crags of these hills thrown up by some terrible volcanic cataclism in the infancy of the Earth, of every shape and form pointing upwards like giant needles, give the island the appearance of some huge petrified, fretful porcupine, or rather from their uniform reddish grey hue that of a monster ant-hill. Not a tree is to be seen anywhere arguing the absence of water, neither eagle nor kite, where one would have thought the place offered excellent nesting ground was visible, and even the sea-gulls seemed to avoid the vicinity. It is a picture of utter desolation. The silence of death seemed to brood over the place. The old town, reduced to a mere town-let, the abode of a few miserable fisher-folk, shell-fish gatherers and petty traffikers, stands on the north side of the island, unseen from the sea. Just opposite to it still stand the remains of the fort of the Portuguese, whence they once commanded and lorded it over the entire Gulf and which stood a great deal of battering from the Company's guns, before it surrendered. It is now a dismantled and crumbling heap of ruins, divided from the island by a narrow isthmus or road way, which once evidently formed a bridge.

Some old guns gone to rust and lying prostrate are still there to attest the early naval supremacy of the great power founded by Vasco De Gama in the Indian and Persian seas and to witness its down-fall. How are the mighty fallen! The fishermen now utilise some of these old guns that once for so long defied the power of Persia and laid it under tribute, as they lie overthrown and imbedded in the sand, for mooring their fishing-boats to. The memoirs of John Kinnear, published somewhere about 1820, mention that three of the guns of the fort were carried away by Shah Abbas as trophies and now lie in the castle of Laar the old Persian stronghold of Laristan several miles inland. These bear the names of 'Dom Philippe III King of Spain'; of 'Dom Jerome Azevedo Viceroy of Goa 1617,' and of 'Dom Juan Continho, Viceroy of Goa 1619.' A few ruins of Convents mark the abode in Ormus of a Roman Catholic community in the days gone by, whilst a solitary minaret part of a Persian mosque that has disappeared still standing and used for sometime by the Portuguese as a light house, is all that indicates the existence of the once flourishing and wealthy city and seaport of Ormus, whose wealth and greatness had been proclaimed to the most distant lands and sung by great Poets. The

Old Portuguese guns.

island, however, still offers much mineral wealth for paying exploitation, which is open to the enterprising capitalist. It yields in abundance its valuable red-ochre, called *Gilek*; rock-salt, manganese ore and other similar minerals, whilst it possesses quarries of a dark, hard useful stone, good for building purposes, so scarce everywhere along the Gulf coasts and all over Mesopotamia. In large quantities this stone is now being carried in special steamers all the way to Abadan and Basra and up the Tigris as building material.

CHAPTER XVII.

The Persian Gulf.

The Persian Gulf referred to always as the Gulf *par excellence*, described by Ptolemy as the *Ichthiophagorum Sinus* or the gulf of the Fish-eaters, was known to the ancients in a general way as the Erythrean Sea, a name also given to the Red sea and the Indian Ocean. It might now-a-days be called the sea of the Shahs, for right away from below Jaskh to above Mohomerah, its northern shores, over seven hundred miles in length, are under the rule or misrule of Persia. The Gulf is actually entered as you come from Bombay by the narrow Straits of Ormus, between the long island of Kishm and the outstanding Salama rocks or between the latter and Cape Mussendam. The voyage from Bombay to Basra, partly in the Arabian Sea, but the greater part of it in the gulf has for the cargo-carrier steamer a remarkably zig-zag course, making as it does one of the many ports every other day or every two or three days. The English mail boats going direct to Basra, touching only at Bushire, make the run in seven or eight days. My voyage in S. S. Zaiyanni took nineteen days, which must be considered good and steady progress, seeing we touched all the ports on either coast and were detained at some for want of lighters; but the Zaiyanni is a most excellent sea-goer; other cargo-boats take much longer on the run.

Ordinarily from Bombay one goes West by North to Masket or sometimes North to Karachi and thence due West to Masket. The next tack takes us almost due North to Bunder Abbas; from there Westward to Lingah, thence South by East to Debai, then Westward again to the Bahreins, from where to Bushire a north by east course. Leaving the

The Intermediate Ports.

latter place we go to Koweyt, West by North; then back again, steering somewhat eastward till you get to the Basra Bar and thence after touching at Mohomera due North on to Basra up the Shat-al-Arab. The Gulf is really a huge lake, bounded by vast sandy or rock-strewn shores, with dangerous creeks and shallows and studded with numerous islands and reefs midsea or skirting the land, which make navigation if not very dangerous, by no means easy. Its tides too are variable and treacherous, requiring the ship's Commander to be constantly on the *quivive*. Ages before the Christian era, the Gulf had been sailed over by those great maritime adventurers the Phœnicians, the cradle of whose race legend gives out was at or about the Bahrein Islands. Nearchus, however, the celebrated Naval Commander of Iskander-i-Rumi or Alexander the Great, was the first authentic European to navigate the entire length of this island-sea, starting with the Macedonian fleet from the mouths of the Indus and reaching Babylon or Susa via the Shat and Karun rivers up to Ahwaz after encountering wonderous hazards and difficulties. The next great European to reopen the Gulf to western commerce was Alfonzo D'Albuquerque, whose daring and despotic deeds and cruelties in these regions still form the theme of many a legend and story.

The Portuguese, under this great Empire-builder, having established their power at Maskat, Ormus, Bahrein and Linga, practically held the Gulf under their control. Chardin, the French jewel-merchant, in his most interesting 'Travels in Persia' records, 'the Portuguese possessed the lordship of the Arabian and Persian Gulfs... so much so that the smallest ship paid them toll. They refused to allow Persian goods to be carried to or from India except in Portuguese vessels, or only rarely on especial permission granted and under very hard conditions. For if a Persian merchant came to pray for a permit, they would ask him, "Is it for buying or selling that you wish to go on to India? If the former, our warehouses here contain every sort of goods you may wish to buy. If the latter, then here we are ready to buy your goods. No need then to go to India. If however, you must in any case proceed to India, you must pay us so much for customs' duty and so much for freight and you can then proceed on your voyage."' This tyranny practised in the height of their power, with most arrogant pride, brought on their downfall. 'Pride truly goeth before destruction and a haughty spirit before a fall.' Later when Portugal came under Spanish rule, her Indian possessions were neglected. The contingents of fighting-men, were sent off to Flanders and the Netherlands to fight for the Roman Church, instead of being supplied to India and the Portuguese power thus visibly declined. Persia and the Arab-chieftains soon perceiving this, raised their heads and disregarded the claims and mandates of the Portuguese. The English, French and the Dutch who followed in their train, grew bolder and the Gulf witnessed many a conflict between these European powers for commercial supremacy, the climax being reached when the English (as before related by me) cast in their lot with Shah Abbas and between them drove the once powerful lords of Goa, from their strong holds at Ormus and Bahrein and finally out of both the Gulfs. Beating in detail their Dutch and French rivals and fortified by valuable concessions from Shah Abbas the English obtained an unassailable position in the Gulf which their fleets have ever since sailed over and held as sole masters.

For Centuries the most daring pirates swarmed in and infested the Gulf:—

'Lords of their world and the wide watery seas.'

Grown fearless by impunity, piracy was their approved and recognised business. The western shores of the great Oman promontory, which was their favourite haunt and which they held in force, was long ominously known as 'The Pirate Coast'. When the Turks, after subjugating the Arabs, established themselves at Basra, their fleet did something in an intermittent way to suppress the sea-rogues' depredations; the latter however, long defied all attempts at suppression and it was not till the British gun-boats came on the scene that this scourge of piracy was finally put an end to. These pestilent water-rats, as Shylock calls them, who for so long terrorised the Gulf, are no longer to be met with there and the Arab and Persian coast-dwellers and all who range these seas must bow their thanks to and bless the British Government for the perfect security they now enjoy.

The Slave Trade.

Gun-running.

The slave trade too, which once flourished unchecked in these waters and along the Arabian coasts, has met with the same fate after many a tough encounter between the British marines and the bold Arab slave-dealers, who were largely befriended by the powerful or petty Sheikhs ashore; whilst the paying business of gun-running, lately so favoured in these very convenient localities, in spite of difficulties with the French and other European States, as well as with the many local magnates, who all largely participated in the huge profits, has become a thing of the past, entirely owing to the determined act and watchful eye of the British Government.

The British power is now happily supreme in the Gulf, which is everywhere effectively patrolled by a squadron of the British fleet, and this great waterway between Asiatic Turky and Persia on the one hand and India on the other is completely under British control.

Pax Britanica in the Gulf.

The Gulf enjoys the ever extending Pax Britanica. The freedom of this great commercial route from all foreign and hostile intervention is of course a matter of immense advantage to all Indian trade, and its security should never be hazarded or lost sight of. Once the Turks had a fleet in the Gulf on which the Oosmanlis plumed themselves greatly and on the score of which the Basha of Bagdad used to be styled 'Capitan-Basha.' No Turkish gun-boat is now to be seen or let us hope ever likely to be seen there, whilst the naval power of Persia, once dominant here in the palmy days of the great Shah Abbas, is represented by a puny little solitary, man-of-war or cruiser called the 'Persipolis,' a gift of the Kaiser William II to the Shah, which rides or rots in the inner harbour of Bushire.

Fish.

Fish of every description, abound in the Persian Gulf; plentiful and cheap it forms one of the chief articles of diet among the inhabitants on either coast, who owing to this, have been known to the ancient as the *Ichthiophagi* or fish-eaters. All during my voyage on the Gulf we were almost daily regaled with fresh fish as we went from port to port. Fish too among them fresh, salted and cured in many ways is an important and valuable article of trade. The other and still more valuable source of wealth to the dwellers along the gulf-coasts, from the powerful Sheiks and wealthy merchants to the poor fisher-folk, seamen and the divers, are the extensive and precious pearl-banks or fisheries that line the southern shores from Bahrein in the west to Debai on the east. There are pearl fisheries at Masket, Sokotra, Ceylon and elsewhere, but none to compare in extent and value with those of the Gulf. The gulf pearl has always from earliest times been famous and highly praised and esteemed for its fine texture, its size, its whiteness and its purity and the pearl fishery, the most important item of commerce in the Gulf, besides yielding large revenues to the petty potentates along its litoral, gives useful and paying employment to the numerous fleets of boats, engaged in the business, with their owners, sharers, divers, and crews. The largest of the Bahrein islands with its capital town of Menamah and its sheltered anchorage is the great emporium of the pearl trade of the world. Thousands of pounds-sterling worth of pearls are fished up and sold annually in the Gulf, whilst the beautifully opalescent mother of pearl-shells, found here in vast quantities, find a ready market in all parts of the world. The advent of the Portuguese gave a great impetus to the Gulf pearl-trade, and the word '*Chao*', the Portuguese name for the weight by which pearls have ever since been sold all over the countries bordering on the Gulf, still used there, is a historic souvenir of their trade dealings. The pearl-banks about the Bahrein Islands are the richest in the gulf. The pearls found there are

The Pearls Trade.

esteemed of a superior quality. The great Albuquerque mentions Bahrein as noted for its fine pearls, he writes, 'Seed-pearls and pearls are sent from there to these realms of Portugal for they are better and more durable than any that are found in any other of these parts.'

<small>Pearl Diving.</small> The pearl diving season commences from early April to end of October and is divided into spring, summer and winter fishing, the first and last being confined to shallow waters and the second to the deeper seas. There must be more than three thousand boats plying about the Bahrein coasts alone engaged in this profitable trade. The negroes, originally slaves from Africa, are reputed to be the most expert and hardy divers, often remaining under water for two full minutes; they command a good wage and are well cared for. The diver is ordinarily armed with a small bight of cord, a stone weight to help his sinking swiftly, a horn clip to keep his nostrils closed and has oil or grease well rubbed into his ears. This very simple and primitive method of fishing up the pearl oysters is still persisted in, so wedded are these people to their old custom and practice, although proper up-to-date diving equipment could largely increase the annual haul-up of these precious shells, the best valued of which have their beds in the deeper waters. Mathew Arnold mentions,—

> *'The wet diver plunging all day in the blue waves,*
> *His pale wife waits and weeps on shore,*
> *By Sandy Bahrein in the Persian Gulf.'*

A fifteenth century traveller in these parts describes the process of pearl-fishing:—'They throw down a rope with a stone to the bottom. In the middle of the boat is one of these fishers with a couple of bags round his neck and a large stone tied to his feet, goes fifteen paces under water, stays there as long as he is able, gathers the oysters, puts them into the bags lets go the stone he had at his feet, and rises to the surface by one of the ropes.'

The Buying of Pearls. Pearls in these places are mostly sold wholesale and it is seldom one can get a really good pearl or a few retailed at Bahrein. Moreover as I was told, many French-made imitation pearls are often palmed off on the unwary traveller, so that it is safest to make a deal only through some properly recommended respectable merchant. The Gulf with its extensive pearl coasts is indeed a mine of wealth to all classes of the people who populate its shores, and largely compensates for the general infertility of its arid hinterlands girdled with the desert sands. The Arabs in these parts often say, 'We are all from the highest to the lowest, slaves of one master, the Pearl.' The yearly value of the pearl output in the Gulf is reckoned as something like a million pounds sterling.

Gulf Trade. Fish, pearls, dates, wool, gums, and horses besides pearls are the chief exports of the Gulf-trade, whilst every description of merchantable commodities are brought to the Gulf ports from India, Japan, China, Arabia, Africa and other parts of the world. This vast commerce is carried on of course in the first instance in foreign bottoms—such as the numerous fine liners of the B. I. S. N. Co., of the Persian Gulf Navigation Co. and other steam-ship companies. Japanese cargo-boats are already cutting their way into the Gulf and are frequently to be seen in its waters. The little Jap is a pushful competitor. The coasting trade however, is still largely carried on by means of the numerous stout-built country craft; huge, ungainly, lumbering, they are, yet are they found to suit the means and the needs of the land and the people. Most of these boats that one sees in the Gulf harbours or meets at sea, though very primitive as regards shape, build, masts, sails, oars &c., are thoroughly seaworthy and serviceable for the business they are put to, keeping in mind of course, Franklin's saying:—

Coasting Boats of the Gulf.

> 'Vessels large may venture more,
> But little boats should keep near shore.'

I should fancy (and I don't think I would be far wrong) these boats are of the same make and fashion as those that carried materials for Solomon's temple in the far far days of old. Made of well-seasoned wood, long pointed shape in the bow, broad-beamed, high at the stern, the interior economy of the ship, as regards sleeping, cooking, toilet &c. is of the crudest, simplest and cheapest, whether *batel or bagalow*, or *dhow* or *mahilah* they are still all equally primitive and very much of a like pattern.

It has been a long standing boast that in all matters nautical the Englishmen are the first of seamen, the Dutch only come second and the rest are no where. This certainly does not apply to the Arabs of the Gulf. In spite of the Islamic anathema, '*men nezel el bahra morreteyni f kad kafer,*' (Who goes twice to sea is a very infidel) the gains of commerce have tempted and turned the maritime Arabs into venturesome, trustworthy and capable mariners, those of Bahrein and Koweyt being especially so distinguished. The Arab boatmen who have at all times sailed and still sail these ships I have above described have a deserved reputation as bold and skilful sailors, used to running sea risks, and I expect if and when caught in one of the tremendous gulf-storms, they are likely to weather them or go under with that philosophic calm or indifference which finds current expression in their ever-ready '*che-kunam.*'

<small>The Arab Boatmen.</small>

In these primitive and to all appearance crazy vessels the bulk of the coasting trade has been from earliest times and is still carried on from Basra right down the Oman coasts to Masket, Makala, Aden, Socotra and even as far south as Zanzibar on the one hand and on the other hand by the Persian coasts to Karachi and the Kathiawar ports and even to Bombay. The very early connection of these Arab coasters with Bombay is still to be found in what was once the island of *Al Oman* which the Tommies quartered in Colaba have turned into 'Ol Woman's Island.' In ancient, yet well within historic times, these same Arab seamen in these same old-world boats rounded cape Comorin and founded a kingdom in far away Java, established the Mahomedan religion in the East Indian archipelego, and for some four hundred years monopolised the rich spice trade and with Basra as their head quarters furnished Europe with the much prized products of the Spice Islands till ousted by the covetous and close-fisted mein Herr from old Batavia, with his unchanging policy of 'giving too little and asking too much'.

CHAPTER XVIII.

Lingah or Linjah.

The great storm I have described having abated, about 10 p. m. we weighed anchor from Bunder Abbas. Our Captain had a *Mauvais quatre d'heure* in getting clear of the huge baggalow which had just foundered by the side of the Zaiyanni, the heavy mast of which half out of water waved and wobbled this way and that, shaken by the still tempestuous sea, and there was a chance of the boats rigging getting foul of our screw. We however steered away clear of the wreck and soon fairly entered the Gulf, between the island of Kishm and the Salamas, passing the small island of Hanjam, which stands close midway to the South of Kishm.

<small>Leaving Bundar Abbas.</small>

All the mail boats between Bombay and Basra touch at Hanjam to carry or drop mails for and from Bunder Abbas, Linga, and Debai, which places the mail-steamers ordinarily do not touch. Hanjam is admirably situated just at the narrow entrance into the Gulf and if in British hands could be turned into a second Perim to shut off effectually all hostile vessels coming into or getting out of the gulf.

<small>The Island of Hanjam.</small>

Soon after sunrise on the 13th December we came to anchor in Lingah roads or harbour, which is pretty well land-locked between the out-jutting headland of Cape or Ras Bostana and the Western end of the Kishm or long island. Lingah with its long array of white houses made more prominent by their curiously contrived high-built *badgirs or breeze-catchers*, is really a pretty little town, forming the port of the large Persian southern province of Laristan. Close at its back stands the Lingah Peak, 3,000 ft. high, which with the Charak mountains to the

<small>The Town of Lingah.</small>

westward and the lovely blue sea in front, gives the place a very picturesque look. Up to 1898 this fine port was in Arab hands; since then it has become Persian by force of arms. On our arrival, after the previous nights stormy weather and rain, we had a delightful, bright day with a cool refreshing wind; the sea still a bit choppy, sparkling in the sun, and Lingah looked very inviting, so that as soon as those picturesque ragamuffins the *Mazduris* were aboard and set to work discharging cargo, the Captain and I, accompanied by Dr. Johnstone, the medical-officer of the Port, went ashore and had a regular day of it, tramping about the curious little town. We landed in front of the Governor's palace, a very unimposing tumbled down building, before which loitered some customs-guards and an illclad, out-at-elbow, Persian soldier was exercising a squad of miserable convicts, who were made to pound mortar in the most primitive and leisurely manner imaginable. First we went and paid our respects to the British Consul at the Consulate, which is a decent rambling roomy building, flat-roofed as all Persian houses. The Consul, Mr. Mongavan, received us very civilly. He gave me a book of amusing Anglo-Indian sketches, and the Captain having done the business he had come for, we said good-bye to the Consul and with the good Doctor, as our very able cicerone, we sallied forth to do the bazars.

CHAPTER XIX.

The Bazaars about the Gulf.

This was my first view of the interior of the famous Persian or Arab bazaar, which it is part of a travellers' business to visit and which most visitors to Persia, Syria and Arabia never fail to extol or execrate as the case may be. I have seen several other bazaars since and it struck me from what I saw and from all I have read that all these Asiatic emporiums or rendezvous of trade must be built on very much the same plan and model and conducted on the same lines, from Damascus to Teheran and from Tabriz to Maskat. It's a case of *ex uno disce omnes*. Large or small, some are better built than others, all are most interesting, handy, and convenient all are uniformly dark and dirty, only some have the distinction of being more so than others. Their construction is on quite a dædalian plan, with intricate alleys, lanes and passages vaulted over and running in and out of each other at all angles so resembling a maze or a Roman catacomb, that any unwary stranger might easily get lost, if not led by some guide acquainted with them.

The one at Lingah is the most decent I have seen, not so large as those at Bushire, Bahrein, Koweit or Basra, it is extensive enough and compact with a labyrinth of streets and gullies, vaulted over and lined on either side with shops, or godowns for all description of goods and wares, from the precious Persian carpet from Tabriz or Kerman Shah, to a rotten Japan-made fan or tooth brush. Every such shop has a front verandah or large door-step on which squat the merchant and customer, making their bargains. The interior where the goods are stored or stowed away is generally unlighted, uninviting and dingy, the articles being fetched out piecemeal and

The Bazaar at Lingah.

The Shops.

exhibited to the purchaser. Dr. Johnstone seemed to be quite at home everywhere we went and a *persona grata* for everybody greeted him with much civility. Being a connoisseur of carpets, he took us to several good shops—where we were shown some really handsome articles, but the prices, owing to the present great rise in the value of the Persian *kran*, which is the local monetary standard, were just prohibitive and gave us no chance of making a bargain, however much we tried. The dealers were polite, spread out carpet after carpet before us to see or choose from; rich carpets, beautiful carpets, trashy carpets, but cared not to abate a jot. The War is of value to them undoubtedly for all caravan traffic from the interior is at a stand still, and so the dealer can command his own price, and choose his own terms for the goods he is master of. Besides the shops, there were there to be found properly assigned quarters for butchers and poulterers, for artizans of sorts, such as carpenters, black-smiths, silver and copper-smiths, makers of weapons, man-milliners, *kolah* and shoe-makers, coblers, tobacconists, etc., whilst cookshops, confectioneries and vegetable and fruit-stalls and several bakeries with steaming ovens and khavakhanas are interspersed at convenient corners where sweet-meats and hot and cold ready made meat-dishes, bread and biscuits, sherbats and coffee and drinks of sorts could be had at all hours to regale and satisfy the inner man or to provide domestic wants and comforts. We made a prolonged tour of the Lingah bazars, much interested amidst these ever moving and interesting scenes. Except just at the noonday hour of prayer, when all business is religiously suspended, Arabs and Persians, Lingahites and strangers, buyers and sellers, idlers and loiterers, visitors and citizens crowded the place. Dervishes and beggars, who claim exemption from all worldly labour or pursuit on the score of their special sanctity, with strings of beads round their necks and wallets in hand or without them, prowl about and intermix with the rest with all the privilege of brahamine bulls in Benares or Mathra. This peculiar gentry *bipedum nequissime* unwashed, ill-accoutred in raiment that is far from savory or free

The Bazaar crowd.

from vermin, go about or linger or stand as the humour seizes them, calling for alms with recited blessings or muttered curses, with no one to stay them or bid them nay. They are not a pleasant lot to jostle against, but no doubt they added an oriental colour and fragrance and flavour to the place. The great variety of Arab attire, Persian, Beluchi and Afgan costumes all to be seen here was curious and bewildering. Every tribe and class of *beni-this-and-beni-that* was represented by distinctive head-gear and outer garment. Some carried dirks or large knives, with handsome horn or ivory or silver filigree-work hafts, struck in their belts or *camerbands*; a very few Persian *gens-d' armes* with rusty matchlock or rifle in hand police the place and moved about in a leisurely unobtrusive way, or stood by or rested at corners. It was a pleasant point to remark that in among all this heterogeneous mass of people there was no brawling, scuffling or complaining; good humour, civility and silence prevailed everywhere.

Women in the Streets.

Women there were seldom to be seen about. A few, likely of the middle or lower classes, were met with, but so muffled up and whimpled in black as to give one no idea of their figure or features. One has to take their gracefulness and beauty entirely on trust or credit. The Persian, thus deprived of the sight of the fair sex, amuses and consoles himself with the saying which I have sometimes heard.—

'Basa-Kamat-i Khoosh
Ke zir ehader bashad
Cho Baz me-kooni,
Mader-i-mader bashad'

which being interpreted means, 'Many a beauty you fancy walks under the *Burkha* sheet, but if you pull back the covering you see perhaps your mother's grandmother.' In Lingah as in other places all along hereabouts there is evidently little or no schooling, for I saw the children about at all hours in the bazars and other-where. They are a delightsome lot.

The Native Children. Boys and Girls, with little to distinguish them by their clothes, grown-up and little toddlers, chubby, rosy, healthy, laughing, frolicsome, dressed-up or in undress, shod or shoeless, it was a pleasure always to watch them. I would address them some funny remark and they would giggle and stare or scamper away. These characteristic bazaars are not only the marts for business transactions and shopping of every sort, but are the general rendezvous for various purposes; for exchanging gossip, for social aminities, 'for eating the air,' and killing the time. Within the compass of the bazaar is also the principal mosque of the place, an unimposing building, without any minaret which may seem curious for a Persian town. It may be mentioned that along the gulf coasts the mosques are invariably without the usual graceful minarets one sees in other moslem countries. The reason is that formerly in most of these places especially on the Arab coasts the Wahabi held sway and his strict and strong puritanism abjured minarets and all church-ornament.

CHAPTER XX.

The Doctor's House at Lingah and other items.

We rambled about the Bazaar and by the busy customs' jetty and the beach, amused and interested, till our legs were near refusing their office, so we adjourned to the Doctor's house for rest and refreshment. Dr. Johnstone's abode is a very large straggling edifice very much out of repair. The Persian clearly has an aversion to repairing. The doctor is still a bachelor and his living rooms were fairly habitable, where he made us much at home. The staircase that took us up was a perfect ruin, which his polite landlord always promises and puts off repairing for want of a propitious hour. Going up was difficult and coming down was dangerous; with my one damaged leg when I reached the bottom without harm, I felt comforted and blessed my luck. In the inner open court-yard such as almost every house here possesses the doctor cultivates a small patch of a kitchen-garden and showed us his few square feet of struggling lettuce, onions and parsley with just and becoming pride. The doctor's house stands at one end of a large irregular quadrangle, with the back of the Governor's so called palace at the harbour end. The Consulate premises on one hand and some large houses, several in chronic disrepair, on the other. The place might be turned into a handsome place of public resort and recreation, but the Persian, I fancy, is impervious to any mere altruism of this or any other sort, and so the place rough, uneven, roadless, treeless is used as a dumping ground for garbage and refuse and abandoned to the boatmen to dry their sails or mend them, stretched out anyhow and all about. Not a tree is to be seen and the glare is intense.

Here in one corner we saw two large masonry built shallow

The Water Supply. circular cisterns, with low vaulted roofs. These are called '*Birkeh*' or little wells and are a peculiarity in all this part of the Gulf. They serve as reservoirs for collecting and storing the rain water, which is what the people have to depend on for their drinking supply. Many such are built in different parts of the town. The same system of water supplying obtains too at Bunder Abbas, Ormus, Bushire and other towns along the north coast.

Some five miles out to the east of Lingah is Kung, along the sea shore, a sort of pleasure resort where still stands, **Kung.** though of course in ruins, an old Portuguese fort. It is reputed to be a very pretty spot. The few Europeans who have to live at Lingah procure themselves some diversion by occasional picknics to Kung. We were unable to visit it, as we were booked to leave Lingah that night. Thanking Dr. Johnstone for his kindness and bidding him good-bye, we rowed back to the Zaiyanni before sunset. The harbour was crowded with sailing boats and coasting craft variously shaped and sized. Some of these were of curious build, with high poop-cabins having well varnished wooden venitians at the stern, prettily ornamented. It was a lovely evening, but a trifle too cool as the Shimal was blowing fresh and chill. The cargo discharging was not completed till after nearly 10 p. m.

CHAPTER XXI.

Debai.

At 11 p.m., we left Lingah. The Shimal or cold north-wester, which had been blowing all day, now increased to something like half a gale and kept it up all night. The sea was a bit playful. Our course was now, almost due South, with the famous 'pirate coast,' once a forbidden zone, on our left. A short way out we passed close to the Tambs, twin islands, on the larger of which there is a lighthouse.

Further on we were within sight of the large Island of Abu Musa, formed of volcanic rocks with several high peaks. It affords some good pasture ground, where the horses and camels of the Shaiks of Sharjah and Debai are sent every wintertime for such grass cropping as they might get. The coasting-boats often find shelter here in rough weather, and the place is said to abound in wild ducks, rabbits and other game. The sailing-boats that often put in here under stress of weather, are held up for two or three days at a time whilst the rough weather lasts. Palgrave was weather-bound here for several days and seems to have enjoyed himself. Considerable local trade is carried on this coast in country craft.

Abu Musa.

The wind had gone down somewhat, but there was a great sea on as we dropped anchor in Debai Bay at 7.30 a. m., about two and half miles off the little town. A heavy surf was breaking on the long stretch of sandy shore and the weather conditions were such that no business was done that day. After much knocking and tacking about, the shipping agent's man got aboard and though our Captain stormed at him to send over lighters and he glibly promised compliance with much interlarding of *Insh'allah,* no boatman cared to put off from shore in that choppy

Debai Bay.

sea, with the wind rising again and blowing hard in-shore. So we had to lump it and wasted the whole day idly watching the pretty waves and gazing at the far stretching gleaming sands that bound the low-lying western shores of the great Oman promontary.

Debai or Dobay, is a small Arab town with considerable outlying territory, situated on a long tongue of land, facing the fine bay and having at its back a very large *khowr*, a sort of inland lagoon common in many places in the Gulf, which, entered by a narrow inlet, affords safe harbourage in stormy weather. This gives Debai the look of a city overlooking two seas and as seen from the ship it really makes a pretty picture, with its long row of white houses, its Sheik's castles and palaces and its *bad-girs* that look like minarets, and might be taken for chimneys. The distant hills to the South of it, with the high *Jib-el-Ali* for a back ground, and the numerous date-palm groves that flourish in this part of Oman, made a *tout en semble* that was very picturesque. Debai is one of the larger of the pearl-fishery stations and is ruled over by a truculent Arab Chief, who measured swords a few years back, with no less a power than his majesty of Great Britain. It was during the recent gun-running and the raiding of the gun-runners which made things very lively in the Gulf, that a British gun-boat chased a gun-runner into Debai bay, landed a party of blue-jackets and came into contact with the Shaikhs armed retainers and a mob of local hooligans. There were some casualties on both sides and a pretty to do as may be imagined. Some four hundred guns were formally delivered up, much more were secreted and carried away as may be assumed, and as the British did not care to proceed to extremities, the Shaikh was thought not to have altogether come off second best. The affair was looked upon as something of a compromise and honours were divided. Since then the little shaikh has been more truculent and pretentious than ever and no non-moslem is now permitted to land at Debai without special passport, and as there is not even a vice-consulate stationed here, the absence of the Union Jack, the

The Town of Debai.

A scrap with the Chief.

familiar symbol of British might, from the shores of this Pirate coast lends some colour to his shaikhship's vaunt that he has withstood the English. I much wished to go ashore inspite of the Shaikh, in my Arab costume, but was dissuaded from doing so and the heavy sea and want of boats were arguments that could not be gainsayed. Towards night both wind and sea went down, so that very early the following morning, well before sunrise, a fleet of lighters swarmed round the *Zaiyanni* with a full complement of *majuries*. The Debai cargo was smartly discharged and soon after noon, our anchor up, we left Debai, seated midst her sands, and date-palms and her surly chieftain with swelled head, behind us about 5 p.m. We passed within sight of the Island of Seir abu Neir or Abu Muh. Many of these islets the voyager sees in the Gulf, they are always interesting to sail by, though not by any means pleasant to run into.

CHAPTER XXII.

The Bahrein Islands.

The passage from Debai to Bahrein is the longest on the Gulf from port to port and the *Zaiyanni* did it well within thirty hours. The weather was cloudy and a pretty high and cold head-wind blew all day with just a drizzle of rain as we gained our destination. Between two and three p. m. the day following our departure from Debai, we sighted the Bahrein coast on our left, with its long succession of low coral reefs and islands stretching for miles towards the harbour-mouth. Date-tree groves covered the islands. The entrance to the harbour or roadstead is between two buoys, one of which carries a red light after dark.

At 5-30 p. m. we came to anchor in pretty low water some three miles opposite the two largest Bahrein Islands. It is well to time arrival here before sunset as the approach to the harbour requires very careful steering owing to the long range of coral reefs, shallows and unreliable tides. As we came close in, the Captain had his work cut out for him and so had the leadsmen. I kept the bridge as soon as land was in sight till the final 'stop her' was signalled and down gurgled the anchors. The coast all along our left as we approached, is low-lying, with numerous detached but flourishing date-palm groves amidst which the village houses could be seen, whilst the roar of the breakers and the beating of the surf revealed the presence of many an islet, reef and sunken rock, which in the dark would be dangerous to sail through.

Approach to the Islands.

The Bahrein Islands are a cluster of seven islands, in between two out-jutting capes or head-lands, which form the entrance to an extensive three cornered fairly deep bay, on the El Hasa Coast of north eastern Arabia, the

The Bahrein 'Heptanesea'

waters of which ebb and flow to right and left of these islands and give them their name which is the Arabic dual form *Bahrein* meaning the two seas. This form of naming places is somewhat peculiarly Arab; Mesopotamia for instance is the exact equivalent of its Arab name for that immense country, 'Naharein' meaning between two waters or rivers, the Euphrates and the Tigris. Of these seven islands, or 'Heptanesea' as they might be classically called, the name by which our Bombay was marked out by Ptolemy, the largest some 27 miles in length, and of great breadth, is the one on which stands the city of Manamah, the commercial capital of the province.

<small>The Name Bahrein.</small>

Next to it, with just a shallow arm or runlet of the sea flowing between, is the island of Moharek, distinguished from the sister isle, by being the resident quarter of the Shaikh and the members of his nobility and of the well-to-do Beherinites. The other islands, grouped about these two, are mere rocks that dot the waters, scantily peopled by a few poor fisher-folk, mussle and edible sea-weed gatherers, and the home of innumerable sea-gulls, cormorants, snake-divers, and other aquatic birds. We stood out facing these towns of Manamah and Moharek and the view towards them off the ship was very pretty. Numerous tall white buildings, amidst which the Shaik's palaces, the residency quarters with the Union Jack afloat above them, the houses of wealthy merchants and the high telegraph and wireless poles lately put up here were conspicuous.

<small>The Island of Moharek.</small>

At sea the day before, we had it gusty and cloudy, but the evening in Bahrein harbour turned out fair and lovely. Though the night was dark and cold 'the floor of heaven was soon thick inlaid with patines of bright gold,' as the great poet says or sings, so that promenading on deck was most enjoyable. The town lights twinkled in the distance.

<small>Evening in Bahrein Harbour.</small>

The ship's agent at Bahrein is evidently a smart man of business. Inspite of the darkness that set in, his manager was on board almost as soon as the steam-horn announced our arrival; and soon after him the lighters got along-

<small>The P. G. N. Co.'s Agent.</small>

side and the *majuris* were at work till late, discharging the cargo of which the ship had brought a large quantity for this port of over 10,000 packages.

The next morning early came the port medical officer and went through the ceremony of examining the ship's papers. He is an important man in his own way. All rolled into one, he is a sort of port officer, the medical attendant in case of need at the Residency, and the personal medico of the Shaikh and his multitudinous household, has charge of a sort of free dispensary and takes such private practice as he can garner in or eke out from among the town Arabs who have however, a religious shyness for western medical science and only resort to it when *in extremis.* This multiplied medico, who paid us his official visit, was a khoja gentleman recently transferred *multa gemnes* from Ratnagiri to this extremely out of the way and uncomfortable spot. He came aboard cased in a heavy and capacious top-coat, his neck swathed in a portentous woolen muffler and a warm shawl went like a cloud round his head. He shivered and coughed and expressed himself anything but in love with his new post. A new man like him, without a connection or a friend, a stranger to the language and in a place that offers no pleasant distraction or recreation and where the house accommodation is full of discomfort, he certainly deserves to have and let us hope he has, a sufficiently high salary to reconcile him to his lot. Captain Ookerji and I on our part looked on the new doctor, a worthy enough young man, as an unexpected contretemps. Before him, the Shaik's doctor here was a Parsee L.M. & S., from Bombay, Dr. Fardunjee Bomylia, a friend of ours, who had stayed on, wonderful to relate, for five years running in this place and had left it unbeknown to us only three days before we reached Bahrein. This was a great disappointment to us and the more keenly was it felt that rather wearied of the monotony of our aboardship fare, which our Zaiyanni *cordon bleu* provided, good enough and ample but a bit too, too stereotyped, we had been eagerly looking forward to regaling ourselves on an exquisite banquet, prepared by

The Doctor at Bahrein.

the doctor's good lady, who had bravely shared her husband's exile all those years in this sort of out of the world place and who is known for her superior skill in Parsee cuisine. It was thus truly a Barmecide feast that we came in for and we had needs to

>'Cloy the hungry edge of appetite
>By bare imagination of a feast.'

However, we were partially compensated for this disappointment, by *a dejeuner al Arabe*, which I describe anon.

The Shaik of Bahrein is a very important personage. He is reputed and in fact is the wealthiest of the potentates who divide between them the Arabian shores of the Gulf.

<small>The Shaik of Bahrein.</small>

His rent-roll is large, and his revenues from customs dues, and imposts on the pearl fisheries are considerable. The Bahreins are an important centre of commerce; practically commanding the head of the gulf, their position is of great strategic value; the Shaik rules over a large population and possesses much influence over the mainland of the extensive el Hasa province. He has made himself and is very useful to the British Government, is created a C.I.E., of which honour he is rightly proud, and to keep him *khoosh* the affixing some day of a capital K. to these magic letters is being diplomatically dangled before his eyes. He is a member of the ancient *El Khalifa* tribe and is the lineal descendant of a long line of Arab Sultans who once ruled over the great province of El Hasa. Ever since 1622 there have been continuous contests between the Arabs of El Hasa and the Persians for the possession of the Bahreins, which were *fortunâ favente* held by one or the other alternately. The Arabs eventually drove out the Persians, but were in turn driven out or subjugated by the Turks, till only the Bahreins remained in Arab hands. Quite in recent times in 1875 the Saiyads of Oman as well as the Turks caused trouble and attempted to possess the Bahreins, but the British intervened. A British gunboat promptly appeared on the scene. The Turks were made to halt, several of the Arabs shaiks were deported to India and the present ruler was placed on the *masnad* and confirmed in his shaikship over these important islands, which he thus holds under the protection of the British flag. The Bahreins have of late become a very important political centre in the Gulf, a British Agent being permanently stationed at Manamah, and owing to their admirable situation have a great future before them now that Bagdad and Basra are in British hands and Koweyt close by is certain to become within a measurable space of time the south-eastern terminus of the Euphratis Valley and Bagdad railways.

CHAPTER XXIII.

How we take to Land at Manamah.

The morning after our arrival the north wind again blew hard so that the cargo lighters found great difficulty in getting along-side and the gangway steps could not be lowered for fear of being smashed. I was however, anxious to get ashore to see so considerable an Arab town as Manamah, so the Captain and I left the Zaiyanni at 10 a. m. The former nimbly stepped down the pilot ladder, but as I have a damaged leg I had to be hoisted up in a huge basket, in which goods that have broken bulk are discharged and was lowered down by one of the ship's derricks into the broad-beamed boat the agent had sent to fetch us. Hanging up in the palm-leaf pleated sack-like basket curiously brought to my mind a picture I have seen, in one of Aristophanes' comedies, where poor Socrates is seen strung up in a basket to make fun for the irreverent Athenian play-going populace. With the tide favouring and the wind behind us, we had the boats huge sail up and enjoyed a most delightful run to shore. It was cold, so that flannel shirts, a warm suit which I used to wear in London during the last winter I was there, a thick top-coat and a tam-o-shanter cap were found most comfortable and the bright morning sun was most welcome. The grass-green waters of the shallow harbour were quite transparent and one clearly saw the many coloured sea-weeds, and the coral rocks at the bottom, whilst the sea-gulls flew over-head and about in flocks, gyrating, poised in the air or skimming the bright, translucent waves that danced and sparkled in the sunshine. All this with the lovely sky above us, the Arab sailors strangely clad, the many country sailing-boats going with the wind or being rowed against it, the strange and novel surroundings, made up a scene not to be easily forgotten and which 'flashes upon the inward eye' so that recalling it fills me with never failing pleasure. This passage to the shore, taking only three quarters of an hour, was all too short. We landed at a roughly constructed jetty in front of the town of Manamah. The Shaik of Bahrein derives a large revenue from the sea customs and could well provide a more serviceable landing place or wharves, where a couple of steam cranes could land the cargoes with a vast saving of time and trouble and disagreements over damaged goods. A wharfage-fee could cover costs. Another thing the Shaik if endowed with any sense and forethought could and ought to do to better the harbour conditions that prevail at present in this place. A couple of steam launches and as many steam tugs, which the Shaik could run on business lines, could be of great service in the shipping and discharging of cargo and conveyance of passengers and save a great deal of time and much annoyance, and add considerably to the Shaik's income. It was a scene of much noise, confusion and activity. Passengers and goods are all landed here pell-mell. The custom's house, a low building with large railed-in compound is within a stone's throw of the busy spot and much was the bustle and the rushing to and fro of men, donkeys and donkey-boys.

Bahrein is celebrated all over the Gulf coasts for its fine breed of donkeys. The stranger is attracted to them at once. They are mostly pure white many of them with manes and tail-tips dyed orange with henna, remarkable for size, speed and strength, and larger limbed than others of their kind in other places. Here as elsewhere in the Gulf the donkey is the universal conveyance and carrier and like the Irishman's pig doubtless pays 'the rint.' The entire absence of all noisy vehicular traffic strikes a Bombayite with a pleasing quietude and a sense of peace. Everybody here has a donkey or hires one and all locomotion is confined to this very useful 'harmless, necessary' animal, unless of course you choose to move on your own shanks. The donkey is furnished with a piece of matting or a rough cushion strapped to his back by way of seat or saddle; bridle and stirrups are considered

The Bahrein Donkey.

mere superfluities; the donkey-boy with a switch in hand runs alongside to guide him, and if the beast is restive, holds him by the ears to restrain any undue frolicsomeness. The people he carries, don't be-stride him but sit with legs dangling on one side or the other. That's the style there. He has an easy little ambling stride that makes the rider quite comfortable. When enacting the porter, he carries bales and bundles of goods, or water-skins or jars strung to each side of him; he carries building materials, sacks full of sand, or anything else that needs transport. The Bahrein donkey, a model for all the rest of his tribe elsewhere, is docile, amenable to his master's switch or shout of command, gives a vociferous chant as the spirit moves him, just to ease off his feelings or by way of salute to a passing burden-bearing brother who returns it with interest. He is really a beauty and commands a good price. During our stay in Bahrein we saw no horses about and but a few camels; but well-to-do people here are known to own many horses; the Shaik has a large stud of them of very prime quality. Horses are largely bred in the adjoining main-land of El Hasa and these are known to be only second in value for beauty, speed and endurance, to that prince of the equine race, the Arab horse of Najed, on the north eastern corner of Arabia. Merchants of course own camels for inland traffic, but the donkey is ubiquitous and equally serviceable both in town and in the mofussil.

When the dutiful donkey is free of a load, either of person or property, his boy lightly throws himself up or leaps with a backward spring on to his back like an acrobat, and swings along at a foot-pace or little trot, carolling, or chaffing fellows of his kith and kin, hailing customers, or jostling passengers with the greatest good nature, and nonchalance, as if that was all in the way of his role to provide a mount or a conveyance. It will be seen the Bahrein donkey is a valued possession, while his keep is not costly. When off duty he indulges in a good roll on his back wherever he finds himself by way of physical refreshment, or stands quietly at street corners nibbling at or

The Donkey-boy.

munching any stray whisps of hay, grass or green garbage that luck might bring his way. He needs no grooming, goes unshod, anything of a shed or no shed does him for stabling, any old drugget or scrap of cloth does for his housing, and he is ready to eat any thing that comes his way in the shape of grub or provender. Refuse of dates and crushed date-stones pickled with discarded dried fish he delights in and thrives on whenever he chances on a few handfuls of these luxuries.

CHAPTER XXIV.

The Town of Manamah.

Of the considerable twin towns that compose or make up Bahrein, Manamah is built along the harbour beach over a mile in length and something nearly as much stretching inland, within which area cluster its dwelling places, its offices and its great bazaars. It is the commercial centre of all these Islands; all business is transacted here. The principal merchants, the commercial and shipping agencies, the British Consulate, all the various offices and the great bazaars with all their multifarious occupants are all gathered in here. The place appeared to be pretty thickly populated. Its numerous dwelling places, and warehouses are closely packed, with roads or rather lanes and byways in between.

The houses or buildings are all invariably white-washed, emitting a trying glare in the sun that for months is cloudless.

The Houses

Many are of two storeys, but all have a curiously unsubstantial and crasy look. Hardly any that do not seem to be out of plumb. Chunam I believe, is unknown hereabouts, and bricks if any are ill-made and sun-baked. The building material chiefly in use is composed of a white conglomerate and rubble of sand and coral rocks dug out of the harbour and coast-line. Many of the houses imitate the Persian style, with terraced roofs, ornamented with open-work stucco balustrades or parapets, hanging balconies, porticos with some pretence to elegance and windows with fretted wooden shutters or sliding panels which give them a pretty look. Curiously enough a number of these houses are in a state of chronic disrepair. All the wood work is of the most primitive. Hardly a door or window fits into its frame or meets its opposite fold without leaving a gaping chink or a crack or a cranny at top and bottom and in between. Oil paint is unknown, and glazing, except in some more pretentious structure is rare. As some compensation for these various defects, which however the worthy Arab or Persian accepts with calm equanimity with his accustomed and consoling '*Che kunam*', I found in some few houses the doors and windows have fan-lights which are glazed with green, blue, red and yellow glass-panes, whilst the generality have very prettily perforated screens or wooden trellis-work window shafts, that lift up and shut down, giving the house its only ornament and helping to deaden the great glare the sun reflects from the whited walls, cools, and also nicely aerates the rooms. Roof tiles or tiles for any other purpose seem to be unknown. All roofs are flat terraces, but which from such as I visited, are so unevenly laid, as to feel like switch-backs. The mason's or bricklayer's plumb and level and the carpenter's plane are clearly rare articles in the Arab's practice of house-building. Owing to climatic conditions in all the lands from the East end of the Mediterranean to the Arabian Sea, the open flat roof has been the fashion from time immemorial. It forms the bed-chamber as well as the parlour or promenade. It is found handy for proclaiming official orders or giving news. The preacher's voice too is often heard therefrom, hence the common expression 'to preach from the housetop.' As a rule the flat roof is protected by a low wall or parapet, which is mentioned so far back as the time of Moses, who directs, 'when thou buildest a new house, thou shalt make a battlement for thy roof.' Whilst the rooms are fairly large and lofty in the better class of houses, the stair-cases are extraordinarily rough, high-stepped and uncomfortable both for ascent or descent. Mostly let into or built against a side wall or corner to economise space they are cramped and crooked with each step quite a foot and half high. One thing peculiar to these Arab and Persian dwellings where blows the scorching *simoom* are the badgirs or ventilating shafts, to provide against the discomfort of the very trying hot season, which lasts for fully five months of the year. Well and skilfully constructed they serve like a ship's wind-sails, to keep the interior cool. In all houses on the gulf shores the arch is hardly known, and the absence of it gives them a peculiar look. Great numbers of them seem built just anyhow without plan or design. This description unchanged applies equally to all the houses I saw at Bushire and other places on this voyage. Although Manamah boasts of something like a Municipality, as I noted from several notices affixed at corners of the bazaar, building bye-laws are unthought of and anything like sanitary principles does not find room in the Arab's or for the matter of that in the Persian's economy of civic government.

Roads in the Town.

Roads in the town, or what does duty for them, and such as you needs must walk on, may be so called out of an excess of courtesy. They are mostly zigzags, uneven, narrow (except just those that divide the main quarters of the bazaars), ill-laid, ill-kept, un-swept and ill-smelling. In many places they are so regularly irregular, so intricate and between such undistinguishing white walls that rarely show a door and hardly ever a window as to require a six months' residence at least and careful topografical training to save one from being in-extricably lost in them.

CHAPTER XXV.

Arab Indifference to Sanitation.

At the landing place and on either side of it which stretches along the beautiful harbour a little effort, a little good sense and a small expenditure of money could convert the spot into a beautiful promenade with seats and shady trees. But the good Arab's æsthetics and ideas of sanitation are entirely negligible, if one may—and really one can—judge from what I saw in every direction in this flourishing and bustling Gulf trade-centre. Western ideas of town-planning and civilised living have not yet penetrated the Arab cranium; however in the rapid changing of affairs that the war is bringing up all over this part of the Asiatic world, gives hope yet and a promise of the bettering of things. *Insha' Allah!*

The Sea Beach. The beautiful Sea Beach in front of the town, where the waves now shine like living emerald, now like liquid turquoise, now with foam-flecked surf glistening in the sunlight, is all abandoned to every description of dirt, uncouthness and ugliness. What roads there are, are mere by-ways, heaped with rubbish and cumbered with goods landed from the ships or about to be shipped. Blocks of building materials, timber, ship-gear lie all about any how, at the peril of the passers by; a number of boats drawn up pell-mell, are moored to the shore with ropes or chains attached to stakes or martin-pikes of a sort in a way that must promote abrased shins and damaged heads provocative of blasphemy and battery. No trees are there that would give shade to the head, or delight the eye; nothing to promote amenity or pleasure; on the contrary everything to annoy the eye and offend the nose. Dead fish, dead animals of sorts and offal strew the place which way so ever you go; such as would create a pestilence but for the wonderfully antiseptic dry air that quickly minimises the nuisances by preventing decomposition. Most offensive sight however, of all and the most horrid, the visitor sees there, are the boatmen and townsmen young and old fouling the shore, all oblivious of good manners and regardless of any consideration for others. This sort of things seemed quite in the order of the day. I saw nobody to police the place and such of the guards that are attached to the custom-house hard by, like Gallio cared for none of these things; possibly having got quite used to them and so are immune to their consequences, and would perhaps miss them if improved away. Man is such a creature of habit, that even abomination ceases to be abominable. The Arab however, more so I think than his rival the Mogal on the opposite shore, is a gentleman. All he wants is a little systematic schooling and drilling and let us hope he will get this in due measure under British rule which must soon now dominate the hinterlands of the Gulf. *Insha' Allah.*

CHAPTER XXVI.

Our Arab Host.

I have been digressing; but it is all a part of my parable. Well, we landed at Manamah; some Arab merchants, who know the Captain, were there to welcome us. With them we marched through the crowded jetty and over the dubious, dirty and devious foot-ways that lead into the town and made for the office of our ship's agent. This gentleman is one of the commercial magnates of the Bahrein world. His name is Essuf ebn Ahmed Kanoo. He is a fine specimen of the well built, dignified and handsome Arab, the true descendent of Abraham's eldest son. He holds the Kaiser-i-Hind gold medal. He stood up to greet and receive us with much cordiality. He has a great regard for Captain Ookerjee, whom he considers the smartest Commander of ships in the Gulf and expressed himself always most delighted to see and receive him.

As we took our seats, coffee, the invariable concomitant of a visit at any hour of the day, was brought in by a servant who held in one hand several tiny cups, which to my disappointment I found were of course Japanese ware, I was expecting something rich in the way of old China or Persian, and in the other hand a brazen coffee pot of wondrous make and shape, that looked for all the world like some uncouth ugly fowl. Diminutive in size in proportion to its head, it has a spout like the beak of a toucan or Malabar horn-bill; out of this dribbled the coffee into the cups without saucers. These singular long-beaked coffee pots, everywhere to be seen in these gulf towns, are kept well burnished and bright and the more of them an Arab possesses the more they display and vouch for his dignity and status. In private houses five or six of these

Coffee and Coffee Pots.

The Arab Coffee Pot.

gleaming round the burning brazier bespeak the wealth and worth of their owners. Saucers are unused and evidently unknown. Coffee of the right sort is the nectar of the Arabs. It is taken hot, thick, black and sugarless; often flavoured with saffron, cinnamon and other spices. It requires an acquired taste, but getting used to it you come to like it and look for it when visiting an Arab's house. There were several other visitors besides ourselves in Mr. Essuf's office, come for business or just dropped in to give 'good day' or how do ye do? Chairs are yet a novelty in these parts, but we were honoured with a couple, which we found were of the old Bombay-make, rather rough, with arms and caned seats and backs. The use of chairs or seats similar to them seems not to have been unknown in Persia and the neighbouring countries more than two thousand years ago, as they are seen pictured in the sculptures at Persepolis. Apropos of this Sir P. Sykes relates the amusing story of a Persian gentleman lamenting the retrogression of Persian civilization, since they in these days, everywhere ordinarily sit on the ground. He was however consoled by the sage observation of another Persian, who unctuously explained that chairs were the sign only of material progress to which Europeans have only just arrived, whereas the Persians have abandoned chairs, having attained to a higher plane of spiritual life! To resume, the Arab ganymede went round serving the fragrant mocha and the strict etiquette for him is to go on replenishing the cup till you hold it turned down. The cup is small and the liquid held is just a thimble-full, so that you might safely indulge in it more than once, as you sit or squat holding friendly palaver. Arab hospitality is such that even a stranger passing by is welcome to come in and unquestioned have a cup or two of the beverage which seems to be kept always on the simmer ready to be served every time a new comer dropped in.

The Custom of Coffee Drinking.

The coffee of Yemen is esteemed the finest and the most prized both as to quality and flavour. It alone is entitled to be called the true '*Mokha*' from the port of its exportation on the Red sea. This is the real *Khavah* or coffee-

Coffee of Sorts.

berry which the Arab *cognoscenti* consider the only one worth the roasting and pounding to make a drink fit for the gods; all the other numerous berries of the same genus are looked upon as merely beans. Palgrave in his Travels describes the Yemen berry as a 'hard, rounded, half transparent, greenish brown berry, which is picked out carefully by skilful fingers. Arabia, Syria and Egypt consume fully two-thirds of it and the remainder is almost exclusively absorbed by the Turkish and Armenian œsophagi, the less generous residue of flattened, opaque and whitish grains alone are shipped for foreign consumption.' The Arab gentleman of wealth and high position and good breed is marked out by the quality of his coffee.

<small>Arab Aloofness and habits.</small> The Arab, of the gulf shores as we know him, is like the Chinaman, most conservative and would much prefer and has for ages preferred to be let alone and isolated from the outward world. He dreads the inroad of foreign civilization, scenting aggression. His needs are few and in the larger parts of northern and western Arabestan wherever Wahabi rule and doctrine prevailed and lingers still, hardly anything like luxury was permitted.

<small>The Simplicity of Arab life.</small> Silks and any other rich attire was strictly prohibited under severe penalties. Wine drinking and even smoking was everywhere forbidden. Even at present when manners have much relaxed, no wine shops are be seen in Bahrein or anywhere in the places round about whilst the tobacco plant is still or was till quite lately, considered an abomination created by Eblis, and is named '*elmukzshee*' or the shameful. Boiled rice with mutton broth and boiled meat, coarse bread and a few dates or curds and cheese for desert, composed their frugal fare; whilst a few carpets or date-tree mats and rough pillows made up their house-hold furniture. The carpet among all the Semetic peoples whether in Arabia, Syria, Palestine or contiguous lands has for centuries been their chair, their sofa and their bed all in one. This fact readily explains how the paralytic would 'take up his *bed* and walk,' when so bid to do by Christ. He had only to roll up his

carpet and shoulder it. They had then no four posters, nor even *charpoys*. Western penetration of these latter days, peaceful or otherwise, has however, been gradually undermining the former puritanic simplicity of the Arabs domestic economy. Arabia now a days is becoming full of new needs and modern appliances. I made especial note of this when visiting Arab houses and offices in the different places I landed at in or about the Gulf.

In the cool and spacious office of our Manamah host, I saw (what must still be taken as novelties such as Mahomed ebn Abd-el-Waheb the great founder of Moslem puritanism, would have abjured and denounced) office desks and chairs used by the clerks, presses for duplicating correspondence, a type-writer, wall-calendar in English, an American clock or time-piece, an iron safe of the newest pattern and withal a Portuguese or Eurasian clerk imported from Bombay, to look after the English letters. In former days door-locks and keys were huge and unweildy made of wood or the clumsiest iron-make. These keys were often some two feet long and so large that they could not be pocketed, so had to be threaded in a long string and fastened to the girdle or carried slung from the shoulder. 'Mais nous avons changé tout cela'.

A Modern Arab's Office.

The old Arab world is in for a change all round. There are now to be seen locks and keys of European and American make. In several of the Bazaars hereabouts, I saw Singer's sewing machines for sale and some actually being worked by the Arab man-milliner.

New Needs and Requirements.

Mention being made of an American clock reminds me to make mention of the quite eccentric way that time is kept in these countries about the Gulf, and my puzzling over it was only abated when on inquiry I was told the Arabs in these places and elsewhere I suppose where their rule holds good, begin counting the hours from sunrise to sunset so that when we have 6 a.m. their time-pieces (if any) point to 1 a.m. and at noon with them it is 6 o'clock, whilst it is twelve o'clock at sunset. How they managed it at night time I missed ascertaining. This method of

Arab Time.

measuring the sunny hours struck a stranger though he came from Bombay as rather topsy turvy and muddling.

Among other modern changes in these countries bordering on the Gulf, tobacco smoking is now universal and very much in evidence. The insidious cigarette of Turkish make is generally indulged in. The old and more wholesome *nargileh* is not so commonly seen. The better class Arabs take to good cigars, whilst of late owing to the war having shut off all trade from Baghdad and Cairo, a home-made cigarette of a long and peculiarly funnel-like shape, composed of a considerable admixture of coarse Indian tobacco, is *faut de mieux* largely used by high and low. Our Indian tobacconists might turn their eyes this way up and about the Gulf and do very good business, I should think. I saw no wine-bibbing, in these ancient lands of the Koran, that have yet remained detached from Western 'Kultur,' at all events in the Western and southern borders of the Gulf.
<small>Tobacco Smoking.</small>

No wine or liquor shops are to be seen in the bazaars. It will I fear, not be long however, before the beer-bottle and the 'water of life' of European living, will find their way in as heralds and harbingers of western civilization and approved sociability. In spite of the strict observance of the quoranic tea-total rule, no doubt much forbidden liquor is privately consumed. Many good men and true of the Moslim pursuasion who visited us on boardship showed quite a cultivated penchant and partiality for the Scotch brew and took it good measure without very much of the alleviating lymph. A change is certainly coming on in these long secluded lands, with the change of times, affairs, and circumstances, and the leaven of western ideas and practice is bringing in a new and wider view of men and things in these old-time conservative lands of the isolate Ishmaelite and of the wild Wahabi, that have for centuries passed been as it were *purdah nasheen* from the rest of the world. Whether this new 'angle of vision' and these 'ringing grooves of change' will be all to the good remains to be seen. *Nous verrons.*
<small>Wine Drinking.</small>

CHAPTER XXVII.

The Bahrein Bazaars.

Our host Essoof Sahib Kanoo pressed us courteously to stay and take breakfast with him and whilst it was being prepared, we were put in charge of one of his nephews to take us about to do the town. Our guide spoke Hindustani fairly and something of English too. He took us for a long promenade in the very extensive bazaars of Manamah. I have already described the bazaars in a town on the gulf coast and the description stands good for most of them. The Manamah bazaars have no distinguishing feature. Some of the mazy roads and lanes are vaulted over, but the larger numbers are just stretched over with dried or drying thatch and crumbling palm-leaves, which keep the place cool, thus sheltered from the sun. Luckily the rainfall here is very scanty else these bazaar footways would be turned into miry agglutinous quagmires so little secure is this overhead covering. We passed and repassed Arabs, Persians, Jews, Negroes and a variety of the sons of Shem, but the Turk to-day was observably absent. Among all this crowd the stately Arab, with his calm demeanor, his handsome person and dignified walk was easily the gentleman.

Though the town is bare of trees and all verdure, outside it are many fine gardens irrigated by wells. The produce of these was to be seen on many of the bazaar stalls or heaped by the way side. Of fruit there are in season pomegranates, mulberries, melons, citrons (which are a speciality of this place), gourds and dates in great abundance. Vegetables seemed to be scarce, but there were lettuce, some sort of beans, and a great deal of lucerne. Lucerne is extensively grown and forms the main provender for horses, asses, and camels. I was surprised to see

Garden Produce.

a ragged Arab quietly pull out a handful of this green herb and munch it in a leisurely way, as if he rather liked it.

Besides dates and fish and a coarse sort of vermiceli, which make the staple food of the people along these shores, the *Behrinites* are said to add to these edibles, dried, salted and pickled locusts as an extra luxury. Locusts when they periodically come, as they do in clouds, are here welcomed as manna was in the wilderness of Sinai and as a brave lady traveller, Mrs. Theodore Bent writes 'the curse of the cultivator is converted into a favourite delicacy.' I regret to say I did not come across this dainty; at the moment it did not strike me to ask for it. I wish I had. The Mosac law pronounces it to be 'a clean creature for human food.' It was no doubt the common diet of John the Baptist and not the carob bean as explained by some too learned scripture commentators.

<small>Locusts.</small>

The Bahrein date it may be mentioned, is of a superior quality. It is a fair sized, dark hued, thin-pellicled, luscious fruit. Dates are found in the bazaar heaped up in masses on open stalls and buzz with their myriads of flies, like goor or molasses in an Indian shop. Here are kahva-khanas or Arab restaurants, with their satelite cook-shops, fragrant with coffee-fumes and the steaming of kabobs strung on loglets or little stakes. These eating places are worth a visit, even if you are squeamish about sampling the fare. Hottest of blackest coffee and the most appetising (if you fancy them) of cooked meat-scraps well-spiced mutton or beef, decrepit ass or mule, or done up dromedary for choice could be had at all times of the day, whilst dates from the stalls and *halva* and sweets from the confectioner's are ready at hand for desert. The baker's oven too, close by, supplies the thick round rather leathery flat bread by no means undesirable, and a sort of excellent fresh cream-cheese and curds too could be had to provide variety.

<small>Dates</small>

<small>Kava-khanas.</small>

CHAPTER XXVIII.

Sundry Items.

I was keenly on the scent for some articles of local make to take away as a souvenir, but found nothing worth the having. Baskets, mats, small and large hand fans and such-like goods made of the leaves of the all-providing date-palm were the only things in the way of Bahrein curios that were to be seen there and these too by no means of any artistic or skilful make. The Bahreins are known, I was told, for wooden bowls prettily inlaid with silver or shells, in which guests and visitors are treated to a drink of water or curds; but I was not lucky enough to discover any of these. *Koojas* or white earthenware porous water goglets and jars, huge and tiny, shaped like the amphorae with ringed handles, are found piled up in the bazaar, but these are evidently not peculiar to these pearl islands, but imported from the Masket side of the Oman peninsula, which is well known for this class of pottery. We visited some carpet and pearl merchants' shops, but prices were so high and the great chance of being deluded prevented our making a bid.

Local Curios.

There were to be seen a number of shops in the Bazaar of miscellaneous and tawdry English and Japanese goods such as hard-ware, cloths and silks, enamelled metalware, cheap crockery &c., and most of these kept by our polite, patient, pliant and industrious friend the Bombay Borah, who speaking a combination of Hindustani and very approximate colloquial Arabic, manages to do good business and to pull on with his strange associations and among his novel surroundings.

The Borah at Bahrein.

The pushful Parsee has not yet penetrated these 'fresh fields and and pastures new' of the Arabian peninsula, though it is quite on the cards that if things go on as they are doing and promise yet to do, with the Union Jack

Chance for the Parsee.

floating *en maitre* in and over these gulf towns and away at and beyond Bagdad, the enterprising Parsee is unlikely to lag behind. He has a keen flair as we know, for anything that could be turned to cash. He is thus bound to come this way. No doubt he is marking time and these far away ancient sleepy hollows may look shortly to be wakened into something like new life under his go-a-head *savoir vivre*, his prompt enterprise, and his vivifying business adaptability and aptitudes, for the full and free exercise of which a fine field in these parts is surely awaiting this worthy follower of the Bactrian prophet.

As a lively example of the prevailing stolid, stick-in-the-mud conservatism of the Arab of these parts, may be mentioned the local currency, which is still largely carried on in the antiquated rial or Austrian dollar with the impression on it of the house of Hapsburg and the protuberent figure of the Empress Maria Theresa. This historic coin still sometimes forms part of a Parsee bride's marriage presents, or decks the swarthy neck of some Hindu woman. Persian as well as Turkish coinage, however, and a good deal of the Italian lira readily pass current; whilst the Indian Rupee promises to become easily the coin of these realms of the Gulf coasts and it is expected soon to replace and do away with the confusing currency intermixture that at present exists much to the stranger's loss and bewilderment.

Arab currency.

Within the precincts of the bazaar stands the Jumma Masjid. It is the only somewhat imposing building I saw in the town of Manamah, with anything like architectural pretention. It has a saracenic arched gateway ornamented with stucco fret-work, with a low, stunted minaret devoid of all ornament and nothing picturesque or graceful about it, for so it is prescribed by Wahabi tenets. Enough that it serves its purpose of calling the faithful to turn to the *Kibla* and say their prayers five times in the day. The Mosque is evidently an ancient building, and like most buildings on the Gulf-side sadly wants repairing, whilst its immediate environments might well be kept cleaner. But it is hoped

The Bahrein Mosque.

with the schoolmaster, who is bound soon to look this way, will come the sanitary inspector and the scavenger to keep sweet the places both holy and profane.

<small>Children at play.</small> The little children, chubby, rosy cheeked fair little Arabs, interspersed with little sable negroes, boys and girls, were for me, here as in other places on the Gulf, always a source of interest and amusement. They were to be seen on the quay-side and in the streets or on the door-steps in groups. Some well-dressed in full Arab costumes, others ragged and bare-footed, but all mingled and moved about socially as equals. I remarked they had little or nothing in the shape of toys and playthings. Any man, in the new era that is dawning hereabouts about the Gulf, who opens a good toys'-shop ought easily to make his fortune. Here, as later in Basra, I saw that the only <small>Games of boys.</small> toy-game the boys commonly went in for in the streets was the whip-top. Any stick with a shred of string and a small roughly shaped pointed wooden peg sufficed. The corkscrew whelk-shell is also readily used for a whip-top; it is of course cheap and plentious and in the expert hands of the Arab gamin, a veritable street Arab, it gave good sport. Even grown-ups are to be seen indulging in this ancient pastime, lashing their whips and twirling the pegs with great zest up or down street, where the absence of all wheel-traffic facilitates the fun. The hoop and the skipping rope and even the kite is as yet unknown among these little folks.

CHAPTER XXIX.

Bahrein Water Supply.

A notable thing in the Bahreins by which one understands the two capital towns of Manamah and Moharek—is the curious system of fresh-water supply. Seeing men and boys, women and donkeys carrying large jars and goatskins of water along the streets at all hours, and noticing no wells or cisterns as at Linga and other places, I inquired whence came the precious fluid and was informed it was brought from the sister isle of Moharek where along the coast there were living springs of fresh water which supplied both these big towns and their suburbs. It is at Moharek that the Sheik resides, and all the grandies of Bahrein. It is a much prettier place than Manamah and has a better climate, it being more open to the sea-ward. It is indeed the seat of Government. Here it is that there are sources of fresh water, springing up *mirabile dictu* from under the sea. This curious natural phenomenon is found also in some other places. At high tide these springs are deep in sea-water. They are inexhaustible. This fresh water is laboriously got at by hollow bamboos or linen pipes being dug into the springs through the sea-water and the fresh water bubbles up limpid, sweet and free from any saline and brackish taste. Sometimes divers are employed to go down and bring up skins-ful of it. At very low tide, when the sea over these springs is shallow enough, people wade in it and get at the water with skins and jars and so fetch their drinking supply. Everybody avers this water is never impregnated with salt, and is good and potable and indeed is about the only water drunk in the two Bahreins. It is sold at a small price per skin. If the Sheik or the so-called Municipality could sense the thing rightly, these natural fountains could be made

Moharek.

available to the general public with much greater ease and at very little expenditure of capital, provided the proper scientific appliances are set to work. Artesian wells, and steam pumps would soon do away with the hollow bamboo, the diver, and such like cumbersome primitive methods, whilst the supply being collected in reservoirs could be carried across in pipes to the larger towns as well as further inland and there distributed by proper pipe-stands.

In the suburbs of Manamah in the neighbourhood of the twin villages of Rufa'a, about eight miles out, there is a famous fresh-water spring well, called Bir Haneini, the water of which is esteemed superior to that from the sea-springs and so affords another perennial source of excellent potable water for the town. Every morning camels and asses are sent out to fetch it and it costs from two to four annas a goat-skinful. These Manamah suburbs surrounded by sandy wastes are well-known for their fertility, being amply irrigated by wells, which the Arabs believe are fed by springs coming underground direct from the Euphrates. The Sheik and his officials have their country villas at Rafa'a.

Bir Haneini.

Another thing too the Sheik, if he be rightly minded, could do to put an end to the constant vexation and inconvenience, his too docile subjects are exposed to, seeing they have daily business intercourse between these two big island-towns. The arm of the sea that divides them has to be ferried over in small boats, in anything but comfort, whilst wading through at low water on foot or on donkey-back is far from being free from danger, and must cause great delay and inconvenience. This channel could be easily spanned by a light iron or steel suspension bridge, and all the trouble and worry people are now put to could thus be easily done away with. The expense of such a bridge would not mount to much and could be safely recovered by a very small toll for a period of years. This is a perfectly feasible undertaking. I have already referred to the troublesome harbour conditions. Thus there are many things waiting to be done that could be easily

The Channel between the Islands.

What might be done.

accomplished in these important islands for the benefit and greater comfort of the people and for the betterment of commerce and trade, adding at the same time to the Sheik's revenue and the prosperity of the country. But the good Khalifah Sheik is a hidebound autocrat, and Arab style prefers to let things slide, being incapable evidently of keeping abreast of the times. *Tempora mutantur*, but not so the Hasa and Nejdi Arab. As I have before

<small>The future of the Bahreins.</small> remarked, the Bahrein Islands have a great and prosperous future before them, if only their Ruler and his too conservative satelites could rise equal to the occasion and anticipate and provide for what is surely coming. In these regions Turkey no longer counts. The asphyxiating Ottoman misrule is irremediably doomed; Russia is on the right side of the fence; Germany is bound to be rigorously kept out; France and Italy with their hands full in Northern Africa are not likely to trouble claiming any zone of influence here. It is thus easy to predict how with Koweyt under the great digit of Great Britain as the oriental outlet of the Euphrates Valley Railway, which must be in British hands, the convenient situation of the Bahrein Islands must give them rank as the great receiving-house of the future between the East and the West.

CHAPTER XXX.

Dèjeuner à l'Arabe.

Having done the Manamah Bazaars or all that was worth doing, we retraced our steps to Essoof Sahib Kanoo's office. My Arabic *gofté-goo* was yet at its extreme embryo stage, but luckily the Captain was a more practised hand at it and as our worthy host managed to speak Hindustani in a way, having visited and stayed in Bombay, our conversation did not lag. He took us round a large caravanserai sort of godown he has just built, with lines of shops or rooms for stowing away goods on each side, a road or sandy passage running between and opening out on to the beach or harbour. There are upper stories and a connecting roof overhead, making it comfortable for seller and customer and being within a stone's throw of the *Ma'ashar* or custom-house, the place is likely to be crowded with tenants and promises to turn out a paying investment. Our host was most diligent in his courtesy, he would have us visit the flat roof of this great building. We had to mount to it by a narrow stucco staircase, imbedded in the wall, as is the fashion here, the high steps of which took my breath away, and required the muscle-power of an athlete's knees and ankles. But the view from the top amply rewarded our unwilling exertion. The entire harbour panorama, in the clear air and under the speckless blue sky was most beautiful. In front of us the shipping with the Zaiyanni conspicuous among them; the numerous native boats with broad white outspread sails plying from ship to shore and *vice versa*; the pretty island of Moharek on our right, with its fine (as they appeared at a distance) palaces and the residency quarters, and on the left the long stretch of the white-sanded Bahrein shore, studded with palm-trees that surround the villages and ending in the

<small>View over the Harbour.</small>

distance with the ruins of the Portuguese fortress that from here erst commanded the Gulf. Going down the precipitous stairs with luck on our side, our host escorted us to his private house which adjoins his office-quarters. There was a sort of central courtyard, and alongside of it was one of those break-neck stairs of the usual Arab fashion. Up these we went and reached the first floor or upper chamber, after passing over a low terrace and mounting more steps, we came to the door of what was doubtless the door of the dining room, or *Kahavah Khana*, or reception room. A couple of Arab attendants met us here with flat metal basins and *abtabas* or ewers shaped like an English coffee-pot only much larger and longer in the neck and spout. Having washed our hands and dried them on towels, which seemed to come from a Bombay mill, and having left our boots outside, we were ushered into the room. Our host, be it said, pressed us not to remove our boots, but we preferred to comply with the custom of the country, and a very sensible custom it is. A large square room, with many doors and windows topped with coloured-glass fan-lights, severely simple and entirely devoid of furniture; on the entire floor was spread a beautiful carpet, with a number of pillows or bolsters ranged round to rest one's back against. In the middle of this was placed a large circular date-leaf matting and on it was a huge circular metal tray heaped with slightly saffroned boiled rice steaming hot. Round the rice were arranged a number of small and large plates and saucers full of cooked viands, composed of meat of sorts and vegetable ragouts swimming in rich gravy. These dishes are very much like those we Parsees are used to. Knives and forks and napkins were absent but the large, circular, flat, unlevened Arab bread did duty for all these. With pieces of it one readily scooped up meat and gravy and deftly conveyed the same to the mouth with ready fingers. For a Parsee this was no difficult feat. One can have an idea of the size of the *suffra* or circular table-mat, as it may be

<small>Arab dining room.</small>

<small>An Arab breakfast.</small>

called, when I say that round it were gathered some twenty diners, consisting of ourselves, our hospitable host and a number of his clerks and retainers and we were by no means crowded. Round this we squatted tailor-fashion and with a general '*Bism Allah,*' the Moslem's grace before meat, fell to on the plentiful repast that was spread before us, our appetites whetted by our long morning's ramble in the keen Bahrein air. We enjoyed the meal amidst the novelty of our surroundings. The Captain and I were providently provided with separate plates in which we sequestered *quantum sufficit* of the rice soused with rich gravy for our own individual use; the rest of the company plunged their right-hands with gripping fingers into the mountain of rice and helped themselves *ad libitum,* mingling the rice with gravy or whey poured or sprinkled on to it with fingers or scoops of the cake-like flat bread, which latter so soaked of course made a toothsome morsel or sop not to be despised. Our good host, on courteous hospitality intent, plied our plates from this dish or that with his own hands. We might have liked to dispense with this honourable attention, but accepted it as men of the world with polite expressions of thanks and gratification. By way of desert we had rose-flavoured *falooda,* a sort of very palatable blanc-mange, cream cheese and the luscious Bahrein dates. Our host showed us the correct Arab style of eating dates. He took a few of them, and like little Jack Horner, 'put in his thumb and pulled out the stones,' stuffed the vacuum with little hunks of soft cream cheese, well jammed in with his honourable fingers and actually himself fed me with these toothsome tit-bits. Our Captain sitting on the other side of me escaped this ordeal. This way of treating a guest is deemed the climax of honour at an Arab's board or rather dinner mat. It is a very ancient custom of the Near East, and subjected to it as I was I recalled the intensely sad and tragic picture of the Gospel story, where Jesus feeds Judas Iscariot at the last supper, saying, 'He it is to whom I shall give the sop when I have dipped it,' would be his betrayer. The date so seasoned was certainly nice to eat, though I

Honouring the guest.

couldn't help a sub-conscious protest at this too honorific method of administering it. Dates over-eaten have an irritating tendency, but eaten steeped in rich cream or stuffed with soft fresh cheese *more Araborum*, they are really enjoyable and most nourishing. Having had our fill and washed hands, we remained sitting a while and enjoyed a couple of the tiny cups of hot and hot coffee, just 'to keep it a'doon,' as Scotchmen say on taking the penultimate or ultimate 'wee drap.' After another ramble about the town, our host most politely escorted us to the jetty or pier and bid us good-bye with many expressions of good-will and hopes of meeting again, as we stepped into his boat which had fetched us ashore and was to take us to the ship. Thus ended our very pleasant excursion to the port of Bahrein. We greatly enjoyed the outing and were much pleased with our reception by the friendly Mr. Essuf Ebu Ahmed Kanoo; may his shadow never grow less and his honour and greatness increase! The excellent breakfast he so hospitably treated us to, will ever make a pleasurable vignette in my voyage to Basra. *Mash'allah!*

<small>Good-bye to Manamah.</small>

Going to land took us a little over half an hour, but going back was quite another pair of sleeves. Both wind and tide were against us, so that now nearly the same distance required over two hours to accomplish. But it was nothing unpleasant and we quite enjoyed it. The boat was taut and sound, and the man at the helm quite up to his business. We tacked and turned about in the shallows, now and then running aground or just crunching over the white coral rocks which we saw under the boat in the clear water, whilst the sea roared at the bow, occasionally giving the oars-men a good splash over, leaving the boat all of a tremor. In one long tack we got quite close to the old Portuguese fort that now stands desolate and shorn of all its former greatness. At last we got into the lee of the Zaiyanni and it was not till well after two bells of the afternoon watch that we were once more footing the good ship's deck. The next day we left the Bahreins at 8 p.m. Before

<small>Return to the ship.</small>

The Phœnicians at Bahreins.

saying good-bye to them, it is interesting to note that very ancient legends connect the Bahrein Islands with the Phœnicians, who were the early settlers in this neighbourhood. Not far out of Manamah there are a series of remarkable tumuli, known to the inhabitants as the 'Mounds of Ali.' Several of these were carefully excavated and explored recently by Mr. & Mrs. Theodore Bent and described in Mrs. Bent's work 'Southern Arabia.' It is conclusively shown that the tombs, houses and relics there discovered are unmistakably of Phoenician origin. The old names of some of these Islands too point to this, such as 'Tylos' and 'Arad or Arados,' which are identified with Tyre and Arwad founded later by these same adventurous seafarers on the Eastern Mediterranean shore when they migrated westward from the Gulf.

CHAPTER XXXI.

Approaching Abu-Sher or Bushire.

All night at sea. It was a fine, clear, cold night. The glass on the open deck must have lowered to good 45 degrees. A warm flannel suit and couple of woollen blankets, plus a rough over-all, were none too much to make one just comfortable in bed. Our course now lay almost due north 180 miles to Bushire, and morning found us well in sight of the Persian coast that borders the vast province of Fars and which is bound by low chains of bare, greyish-yellow burnt up, desolate mountains stretching eastward and, as an English traveller describes Persian scenery in another place, there 'was neither bird, beast, shrub, scrub, tree, twig nor human being to break the impressive monotony.' But the sea! The sea was beautiful and the weather serene and cold. It was a perfect day to enjoy a ship's deck and that ship the steady-going Zaiyanni. Early in the day we sighted, miles away to the north, the curious peak of Kuh Khormaz rising 6,500 ft. above the sandy seashore. This high hill looks like a guardian sentinel standing watch and ward over the Shah's good city of Bushire. All my inquiries as to why this mount is so named remained unsatisfied. If Khormaz has anything to do with dates or date-trees, then it is possible this hill in its far-spent infancy was planted with such. At the present day there is no vistage of any vegetation whatever on its ravaged and scarified sides to justify this appellation. Going to or coming away from Bushire for miles along the coast line Khormaz towers conspicuous to the view. On the side of it to the sea there is peace if not plenty, the region being quite bare of trees, but beyond it and over the hills are the ever restless and lawless Tangistanis, the Bakhtiaris and other ravening robber tribes with whom Persia,

Kuh Khormaz.

owing to her feeble and unstable rule, is largely cursed, all prepared for or preparing any devilry that offers a chance of looting, bloodshedding or brigandage. Further to the north-east appears to view yet another lofty peak furnishing a fine landmark to sea-goers. It is known as the Gisakan Bluff. Snow is sometimes seen on its summit, though I caught no sight of it however much I tried to see it with the ship's telescope. As we got nearer, the first building we sighted was the tall melon-shaped cupola or dome of the Imambarra, white as a wedding cake, standing amidst a rare grove of trees; it is conspicuous for miles along the coast, and stands in the suburb called Shabzabad, some five or six miles to the south of Bushire. In this quarter are situated the dwelling-houses of the British Resident and of such of the English and foreign gentry as live here. The Imambarra is the distinct symbol of the Shiah faith which is the national religion of the Persians since the days of Ali, the first Imaum. There are no such institutions on the opposite Arab coast, where Sunnis and Wahabis abound, bitter enemies of the rival Moslem creed.

The Imambarra.

About 5 p. m. as the sun was lowering westward we entered the outer harbour of Bushire. Here stood at anchor H. M. S. man-of-war Juno, the flag-ship of the Naval Squadron that policies the Gulf. The Zaiyanni dipped her colours in salute which was promptly returned by the great gunboat, which ran up a signal that we were to stop. The Zaiyanni had to slow down and circled round the Juno, till an officer from the latter came off in a steam-launch, boarded us, and delivered some secret orders to the Captain. This ceremony lost us a good hour, but we just managed to make for the inner harbour and anchored before the tide set in against us, a couple of miles in front of the Town. On one side of us we saw the entire Persian navy riding at anchor, consisting of the single cockleshell of a gun-boat, painted white, the Persepolis before referred to. Owing to some Persian galaday, her masts were

H. M. S. the Juno.

The Shah's Navy.

gay with bunting, among which the Shah's flag, bearing arms of Persia, the lion and the sun, was conspicuous.

In all the other ports we made up to now there is no pilot-service, but here now-a-days a ship entering and leaving the Bushire roadstead, and making other ports on its way northwards has to take a pilot on board. Evidently a needless imposition, for the pilot who was to board us outside the outer harbour delayed coming and the Zaiyanni fearlessly rode in and anchored without him, her capable skipper knowing every square inch of both the harbours, which he has so frequently crossed and re-crossed without being piloted. It was well after we had been safe in and snug enough that our pilot came aboard, a tall wizen-faced, weather-beaten Persian, a very decent, good tempered loquacious old salt, who praised our Captain's seamanship and proffered profuse excuses for not turning up in time. After him came up Dr. Hudson who is one of the two English doctors stationed here, who examined the ship's papers and sat with us sometime exchanging news.

Kuh-Khormaz, which all the day before heralded the vicinity of Bushire as we sailed up the coast, I now saw standing though miles away as if just behind the town of Bushire, lifting his bare and lofty crest like a dark curtain, and the following morning my early rising was rewarded by a lovely sight. The sun gradually uprose behind this notable hill, which stood clearcut against the iridescent East, and cast the gloom of its huge shadow over the harbour and over Bushire City at its foot. Then as the sun topped the pinnacle of Khormaz like a ball of fire, the white city and the burnished glimmering waters that lap its frontage came out beautifully into view, bathed in the slanting rays of the morning light.

Pilots.

A fine view.

CHAPTER XXXII.

Bushire.

Abu Saher, or as it is usually called Bushire, is so called because it is said to be the 'Father of Cities'. Some derive it and it seems a more likely derivation, from what is said to have been its early name 'Bokht Ardesher,' so known in Sassanian times. Ardeshir Papak or Baba Khan, the founder of the Sassanian line of Persian kings was the great hero of his people, for the names of many a town and river and important landmark are derivable from him. The town of Bushire or it may be dignified with the title of City, seeing it is the headquarters of the British Resident and the seat of a Persian Governor, is situated on the western coast line of Persia, on a long low-lying tongue of land, facing North, with its two harbours in that direction. It has a population of some 25,000 souls and is now the seat of the Government of the Persian side of the Gulf under a Resident Governor. It is the headquarters of the British naval squadron, and its importance is further enhanced by being the residence of so high a political dignitary as a British resident and Consul-General. Its sea-borne trade is considerable with India, Arabia, Java and Japan, its exports being chiefly carpets, gums, wool, opium and rosewater. There are here several European mercantile houses, and the principal shipping offices are established here.

There does not appear to be anything of much general interest in its early history. The extensive ruins at Reshire, (a name evidently connected with Ardeshir Papak, the Sasan monarch,) about two miles out of Bushire, show that it had its origin as an early Elamite settlement. It rose into importance in the time of Shah Abbas the great, who aspiring to control the Persian Gulf, selected it as the South-Western port of

<small>Early history of Bushire.</small>

Persia and made it the dockyard of his infant navy. In 1759, the English removed their trading factory to this place from Bandar Abbas and were much favoured by the great Shah. Bushire was the starting point of Sir John Malcolm's famous first embassy to the Court of Persia, to counteract the French intrigues in the reign of Fateh Ali Shah.

The illustrious Elchi and accomplished diplomat is reputed to have introduced the potato into Persia, as a memorial of which interesting fact this edible tuber is hereabouts still called the *aloo-i-Malcolm,* as mentioned in the amusing 'Sketches of Persia.' At Avignon, in France, they have erected a statue to a Persian who introduced into France the cultivation of madder; the Persians might have done the same by Sir John. A propos it may be of interest to mention here that it was on the occasion of his second embassy that the Persian Order of Knighthood was especially instituted to honour Sir John. The manner in which it was created is curious. During his two visits as ambassador, he had become a great favourite with the great Sophie or Shah, who contrary to all precedent and against all the rigid court etiquette treated the Elchi with the most gracious attention, friendship and even familiarity. Some years previous to Malcolm's visit the Shah had created 'the Order of the Sun' in honour of General Gardane, who had come as Bonaparte's ambassador. This order was offered to Sir Harford Jones, Envoy Extraordinary of the King of England. Sir Harford punctiliously declined to accept it, considering its origin. It was next offered to Sir John, who not a whit backward in maintaining the dignity of the Government of the East India Company Bahadur, loyally followed Sir Harford's proud example. The Shah, however, was not to be denied and got out of the quandary as Shahs alone can by especially creating as it were a new order, which is 'The Order of the Lion and the Sun'. The jewelled

<small>The potato in Persia.</small>

<small>The Persian Order of Knighthood.</small>

<small>The Persian Order of Knighthood.</small>

insignia of this now well-known order were pinned on to Sir John Malcolm's breast by the Shah's own august hands; and the illustrious Elchi was at the same time dubbed Khan and Sipah-Salar of the Empire of Persia. In this order the Sun no doubt relates back to Mithra whose worship so widely prevailed in the early Persian Empire; whilst the addition of the king of beasts is possibly intended as a compliment to the British lion.

<small>The Persian War.</small> In 1857 when the Anglo-Persian War broke out, Bushire was occupied by the British Indian forces under General Outram. Reshire, stoutly defended, was stormed. The Persian army encamped at Borazjan on the road to Shiraz precipitatedly retired on the approach of the British, who having blown up the Persian powder magazine and not desiring to press on to Shiraz fell back on Bushire. The Persians emboldened by this politic if not strategic retreat, followed up and delivered a strong night attack at a place called Khushab, but were there signally defeated. This victory of Khusab and some successful operations in the neighbourhood of Mohomerah, brought the Persian War to a speedy close. The British too were anxious to conclude peace seeing the troubles of the great military revolt that then broke out in India. During the present great catastrophic war that is devastating Europe, Bushire was for a short time occupied by the British in considerable force, owing to serious disturbances that were threatened under German machinations by the wild tribes that people the hill-country to the east of it. At the time of my visit there were still three Indian regiments stationed there as a precautionary measure, the condition of things being considered still of so parlous a character, that sepoy and soldier were both forbid straying beyond five miles of camp-limits. As to the future of Bushire, <small>Future of Bushire.</small> according to Sir Percy Sykes, whose long residence and extensive travels in Persia gives him complete first-hand knowledge, this old seaport as time goes on is likely to sink into insignificance, as its rivals Mohomerah in the west and Bandar Abbas in the east are bound to rise into greater importance, and this

looks particularly likely to be the case, if ever Teheran is connected by rail with Quetta *via* Bandar Abbas and Isphahan.

CHAPTER XXXIII.

The City of Bushire.

The day following our arrival, the weather being cold and bracing, the Captain and I went ashore in the old pilot's barge and with him as our cicerone we did the lions of Bushire. The run to land in the pilot's broad-bottomed lumbering boat, over the shallow waters of the inner harbour took nearly an hour and then after squeezing in between a number of country boats, which be it noted all bore English marks and numbers, we got out at a tumbled down, ill-built jetty or landing place mud-laden and slippery close to the Customs' house. Having had to scramble over bales of goods which lay promiscuously scattered about awaiting disposal by the customs officials, we managed to struggle out on to the main promenade or marina, which fronts the sea and along which the town is built. Here stand most of the better sort of residences and offices with the Governor's palace, an unimposing building in bad repair; further up is the British residency official quarters with some Indian soldiers on sentry duty at the entrance. The Marina stretches some five or six miles southwards towards Shabzabad, the pretty suburb I have mentioned before, and so called no doubt because it is embowered in a number of large shady-trees other than the date-palm. The French, Italian, Russian, German and Turkish consulates are situated along this fine road, with the beautiful blue sea lapping its front. As things are, the last-named two consulates are of course closed and abandoned, and their former inmates are known there no more. In French or Italian hands this grand sea-side promenade would be transformed into something lovely and delightful and would make Bushire an attractive winter resort. As it is, the place has an abandoned look;

The Marina.

the road is ill-made and full of ruts and holes, the seashore is strewed with rubbish of sorts and the houses have a forlorn, groggy, dilapidated look. There seemed to be no life about the place. The few Persians and Arabs we met just pottered along listlessly, as if they had no settled idea where they were going to or what they had to do. A few women there were out walking, swathed like mummies all in black, with ugly mask-like flaps that hid their faces, their blue linen baggy trousers tied tight round their ankles, and their feet encased in the clumsy low-heeled *pa-poush* so common in Persia. They would do immense credit if carried in an undertaker's coach following a funeral as mournful mutes. The only relief to the depressing effects of the dullness and colourlessness that met one's view on this fine sea-walk at Bushire, were a few children that trotted alongside their parents or attendants. They looked well-fed and were a pleasing sight with their rosy cheeks, black gleaming eyes, white teeth and laughing faces. We looked up Dr. Hudson in his dispensary which is located on the first floor of a rickety house on the sea-face, and which we had to climb up to over a flight of narrow, portentously steep and dirty steps. We found the doctor busy considering, prescribing for and dosing a number of patients, among whom were a great many women and children. The common complaint appeared to be eye-troubles, fever and cough. It was an interesting scene.

Women on the road.

The Persian children.

Dr. Hudson's dispensary.

Coming out again in the open, we sighted a dapper little man, in full khaki accoutrement with a profusion of belts, shoulder-flaps, a multiplicity of leather straps, buttons, and buckles; his little legs lost in putties and heavy boots with spurs on and riding a gaunt bay whaler far too large for him. A British military swell, we made no doubt, as smart as they make them, and we were agreeably surprised when this potent, petit and warlike seigneur turned out to be my nephew, Captain Heerajee Cursetjee, I. M. S., who was then quartered with

A Parsee Captain of the I.M.S.

his regiment at Shabzabad aforesaid. Since the war began he has seen much active service on the Suez Canal, and then in Galipoli, where he was all but mortally wounded. After spending several months in hospital at Malta and in London, being pronounced fit again for service, he served on the Tigris front and was recently relegated to Bushire with his regiment, which with other Indian regiments were at this time in Bushire to keep in check the Dashtis and Tanghistanis and other equally Iranian gentle folks whose 'constant care is to increase their store' by troubling and harrying the Persian and adjacent Turkish borders. Captain Heerajee has since been on active service again on the Baghdad front, and beyond. I had telephoned to him our arrival and appointed our meeting at the customs' house. We missed him there, and it was by good luck we thus came across him on the Marina. He took us over the extensive Residency quarters, and having tethered his horse there, paraded us through the Bushire bazaars. As I have said before one of these bizarre bazaars, or labyrinthian congeries of roofed-in alleys with their multitude of booths, stalls, shops, godowns, is so like any other in these Gulf towns that the one at Bushire needs no further description and as Chaucer hath it, 'of their array tell I no lenger tale.' We sauntered about in a leisurely way in and out of the intricate lanes and passages, inspecting carpets, old weapons, brass and copper articles, in all which Captain Heerajee acquitted himself *en connoiseur* on the strength of his recent residence in Persia. He spoke the lingo passably well and no doubt much impressed the natives, but we made no bargains as the wily Mogal was intent on doing us in the eye.

In the bazaars at Bushire.

CHAPTER XXXIV.

The Ship's Agent at Bushire.

We next visited the house of the Agent of the P. G. N. Co., Hajee Abdul Russool, *Rais-i-Tajarat* or headman of merchants, in the business quarter of the town. It's a large house of the usual Persian style, with inner courtyard and upper storey. Here the Rais both lives and transacts his very extensive business. He is a gentleman of wealth and of consequent consideration in Bushire. He was proportionately stiff and elaborate in his reception of us. His features, rather dark for a Persian, are by no means unprepossessing though there is more in them of the hawk than of the eagle, betokening great business astuteness and *savoir faire*. Hardly deigning to rise he shook hands with us. He was busy in his office, which was fitted up like any up-to-date office in Bombay, with large writing-table, a swivel-chair, setties, bookshelves, a telephone and spare chairs. In an adjoining room were seen a number of clerks and many attendants, among whom I noticed the Persian office-walas have not yet imported the *pattawala* or *chaprasi*. Whilst the Captain talked business with the Rais and his Mirza, Dr. Heerajee and I sat by twiddling our thumbs, till the bringing in of liquid refreshment gave welcome hint for our departure. In

<small>New fashion in drinks.</small> Arab houses coffee is served in little cups; in Persian houses it is tea or sugar liquified in tea without milk in tiny glasses, or it is sherbet. It would have been nice to have had some delicious Persian sherbet; even the too luscious bohee might have been tolerable; but no, for surely 'the old order changeth giving place to new'—and the Parsee-prepared 'pick-me-up' has latterly penetrated the Persian Gulf litoral, along with other aerated decoctions for which both the Persians and Arabs, eager to be in the

fashion of the day, are contracting a vicious taste. The Rais, therefore, treated us to glasses of 'pick-me-up,' which we had to sip or swallow as each felt the need after our long ramble, and what was left at the bottom I saw the Rais' servants in another room emulously swill with evident gusto testified to by audible smacking of lips. We then took leave of this Bushiri commercial swell, who condescending to shake hands with us, without rising from his office chair, which he occupied as if it were a regal *masnad*, stretched out his hand looking as if he expected us to bow over and kiss it. Exchanging the customary '*Khoda-hafez*,' and bidding good-bye to Dr. Heerajee, the Captain and I found our way back to the squalid customs' house wharf and took boat to return to the Zaiyanni. In this customs' house I observed many notices, which were given both in Persian and French, among these was the frequent '*defence de fumer.*' In Persia, as in Egypt, the better or educated classes use French more commonly than any other foreign language, it having so long been the language of diplomacy. The wind being against us, we had to knock about a good deal, and after making a long detour, reached the steamer which was still discharging cargo, about 4.30 p.m. In order to catch the right tide we weighed anchor at once and steamed out to a position in the outer harbour, dragging along on either side of us a crowd of the lighters, some part-loaded and others empty, a rather delicate operation safely accomplished. Here we shipped our pilot as is now the rule; he accompanied us to Basra and back, pilotage being as I said before, compulsory now over the Basra bar and up the Shat'-el-Arab. We also had to take in here on board a large posse of *madzuries*, to help unload and load cargo at Koweyt, Mahomerah and Basra, as great difficulty is experienced in obtaining proper hands at these ports. At last the full tale of the Bushire consignments being discharged, by 8 p. m. the anchor was up and we set sail for Koweyt.

Leaving Bushire.

Taking aboard Madzuries.

CHAPTER XXXV.

Koweyt.

From Bushire to Koweyt, our next halting-place, we made a good run of about sixteen hours. The weather continued beautifully fine and enjoyably cold. A high chill wind, the rude Boreas of the Gulf, accompanied us all night, keeping the sea pretty lively and fretful. Early in the morning of the 21st December, 1916, we passed close to the Island rock of Khabbar, on which there is a beacon-post. We had now the Arab coast of Nejd or El Hasa full in view on our left, with its endless wastes of bare sand hills and further away on our right to the north-east the wild mountainous region of Khuzistan or Persian Arabistan, with the lofty peak of the Kuh Bebehan in the distance which is easily sighted from afar and is generally covered with snow for a great part of the year. At 11-30 a.m., we were well in sight of Koweyt; the newly-built pleasure-house of the high and mighty Sheik of Mohomerah, a large building gleaming white, is the first conspicuous object to catch the eye. The Mohomerah potentate, often comes here in his steam-launch to spend the week-end. Passing a couple of buoys, which the ship's chart says are not to be relied on, and rounding Ras-el-Ajuza we entered the fine well-protected natural harbour and came to anchor soon after noon, opposite the town of Koweyt where stands the Sheik's castle, prominent among the long stretch of buildings which line the sandy strand.

Approaching Koweyt.

The foundation of Koweyt dates back to very ancient times and like the Bahreins takes its origin from the earliest of Phœnician and Greek settlers or immigrants. It is said to have been the ancient Teredon, whilst the names of neighbouring towns and places, though now much corrupted or

Early history of Koweyt.

changed, go well to establish this old-time origin. Andrasthenes, a companion of the celebrated Nearchus, when returning from Alexander's Indian conquests they navigated the entire length of the Gulf, mentions the island of Ikaros, (now Peludji) off Koweyt, where he says he saw a temple of Apollo, and lower down coast he came to the Greek settlement of Gherrha, the earliest mart between Asia and Europe. Opposite this were found places which he calls Tylos and Arados, where too he writes he saw 'temples like those of the Phœnicians.' Nearchus too mentions a town in this part of the Gulf called 'Sidondona,' and an island which he visited called 'Tyrine,' where he says he was shown the tomb of the more or less mythical King Erythras, from whom it is supposed the Gulf received its ancient name of the Erythrean Sea. Of these ancient settlements no traces now remain, excepting such as have come to light as above mentioned, in the neighbourhood of Manamah in the larger of the Bahreins. These interesting traditions are confirmed by early Greek writers like Herodotus, Strabo, Ptolemy and Pliny the Elder. The land anciently was known as the land of Punt, and its inhabitants were the Puni, from which term no doubt we have the name Phoenician and the word 'Punic' describing them their wars and their bad faith.

CHAPTER XXXVI.

The Town of Koweyt.

The town of Koweyt, in the north-western angle of the head of the Gulf, is situated on the southern shore of its harbour, which is landlocked on three sides. The sea on one side and the illimitable sandy desert on the other. The name Kuvet or Koweyt is the same in Arabic as Kut, now so well-known all over the world in connection with British military exploits, and means a walled town. Already a place of much commercial importance, under the changed and rapidly changing present condition of things all around there it bids fair to rise into still greater value and prominence, as the great trading centre of the future in these parts. It has a population of between fifteen to twenty thousand souls. Its waterway connection with Al Basra at present requires a voyage by steam-boat of between 30 to 40 hours; but standing as it does due south of that great date-port, the intermediate distance by land as the crow flies is very much shorter, and is over what appears a level tract of land that present few difficulties for a rail-road, which now must find its way there sooner rather than later, and make Koweyt its south eastern terminus. Its future prospects are thus of the most promising, and our enterprising Bombayites would be missing a great opportunity if they delay or hesitate acquiring land and concessions of sorts within and about the Koweyt boundaries. Turkey holding as it did Basra, had long been casting covetous eyes on Koweyt and in 1898 made a determined attempt to get hold of it by hook or by crook. England, however fully alive to the sinister consequences had the Turks succeeded, intervened and frustrated the attempt and since then Koweyt with its Sheik are placed under British protection, which spells 'hands off' to all and sundry who may wish to get there. More so than ever must this status be now preserved absolutely without the least loophole, diplomatic or other, for foreign interference or intrusion. The map is changed indeed. All Mesopotamia where hitherto waved the blighting white crescent right down by Koweyt and further to the Bahreins, must now bear the pink hall-mark and sign-manual of British possession or suzerainty. '*Sab lal Hojanahai*'! Let us hope that no idle sentiment, socialistic fad or folly or weakness of statesmanship, or diplomatic ruse or tactical bluffing of any alien power will prevent this consummation! British as well as Indian interests have been growing year by year in the Gulf and along the Shatt. And the Karun, therefore in these regions now and hereafter must British ascendancy be maintained intact and intangible against all comers. The harbour of Koweyt is a spacious piece of water, but with unequal depths from fathoms four to nine or more. We anchored as near in shore as the Zaiyanni could safely go, some three miles off the town, which from a distance made a very fine show with its extended sea-face on which stand the castle, the Sheik's palaces, the residence of the British Political Agent, the Customs' house and a serried row of the usual flat-roofed houses and offices of well-to-do merchants and others. Two steam-launches owned by the Sheik lay at anchor, and the harbour was alive with a great variety of local boats, lighters and country-built coasting-craft. Koweyt is famous all over the Gulf for its excellent boat-building and the strand was crowded with a great number of boats a-building and new boats ready to put to sea. As soon as we were stationary, Mr. Abdul Latif, the Sheik's Commissioner of Customs, Mirza Habib, the Agent's factotum and the English doctor, Dr. Kelly, boarded us and spent the afternoon with us. Soon after them came up the consignees of goods or their men with a number of those black-hulled, heavy-going lighters, which attached themselves on to either side of the Zaiyanni like a school of porpoises attacking a leviathan, and into these our Bushiree *madzuries* without loss of time began discharging the cargo, with the usual hoarse

Koweyt harbour.

Koweyt boats.

Koweyt gentry.

clamour of a babel of tongues, and the thad-thad of the donkey engines, the continuous rattling of the winches and the grinding of the chains through the iron pulleys at the derrick-heads. It was a repetition of the scenes I witnessed at the preceding ports—all bustle, noise and business. The unloading went on till near midnight.

CHAPTER XXXVII.

Ashore at Koweyt.

<small>Abdul Latif, our Koweyt host.</small>

The following morning early, the good man Mr. Abdul Latif came and invited us to spend the day in town and breakfast with him. He is a most charming personality and a credit to the Arab people. Of middle age, stout-built, tall, of fair, handsome features and jolly, cordial, engaging manners, his kindness courtesy and frank *bon-hommie* soon put me at ease with him. He speaks English in a way and Hindustani fairly like many of the Arabs who are in touch with Bombay, so that we got on very well together. Besides being in charge of the sea customs, he is a member of the local Sheik's rather numerous council of elders, and has acquired a high reputation and esteem for ability and integrity. In his capacious harbour boat, reclining on carpet and cushions, we made, the Captain and I, a pleasant sail to shore, landing dry-shod at the customs' bunder, inside a sort of small roughly-built breakwater, bounded by uneven stone-blocks, within which at low tide there is more mud than water. Like most things structural in this ancient land, typical of the unchanging East, the bunder steps and the breakwater walls were more or less tumbled down. Mr. Abdul Latif informed us the breakwater is shortly to be expanded and thoroughly repaired. *Insha-Allah! Spes est si non res.*

<small>The Customs house.</small>

With the worthy Commissioner Sahib for guide, we first visited his office, where we were served with the inevitable coffee. Next we went over the customs house, which is an extensive irregular building so far as I could see, here heaped, there strewn with bales, bundles, baskets, boxes and cases of all sorts and sizes in what seemed to be unremediable confusion. It was ill-ventilated and ill-lighted, with its floor in alternate patches of loose sand and hardened conglomerate. Proceeding thence we made a thorough inspection in and out and roundabout, of the Koweyt bazaars, which are much on the same plan and pattern as those elsewhere I have previously described. Our guide, the Commissioner and Councillor of State, was everywhere met with respectful salutations, which he returned with fraternal cordiality. The butchers' quarters we visited were an interesting if not a pleasant sight, with a display of large joints, that were conceivably come from camels that useful locomotive of the desert past further service. Anything like regard for sanitation here as elsewhere about the Gulf was unthought of and the stench of stale and freshly slaughtered meat and the circumjacent squalor did not invite our lingering here long. Getting out of the bazaars we came upon a very extensive esplanade or open space on south-west corner, where *inter alia* we saw a number of Arab money-changers, each seated in front of an arrangement of several boxes of various sizes and of very fragile make full of coins, with locks and hinges of so primitive a pattern that the veriest tyro in Bill Sykes' profession could pick them with the utmost ease. Mr. Abdul Latif astonished us by averring that so perfect was the honesty of the dwellers of Koweyt, that these local bankers when retiring for the night left these treasure chests where they stood in the open and never a case of theft has been known! I do not in the least bit desire to say 'credat Judæus Apella,' but I just trust that these fortunate bankers of Koweyt are reciprocally above-board in their dealings with these good people. Not far from here are two unimposing single-storied, very plain buildings, on either side of this esplanade, where the Chief of Koweyt daily takes his seat to administer justice, in the forenoon in one house and in the afternoon in the other. Further inside the town is a large fairly well-built schoolhouse, which we explored. It is a square building, with a large courtyard, several class-rooms fitted up on the ground floor with small low desks and strips of drugget or carpet and Arabic texts on the walls, whilst the upper chambers are occupied by the *Akhoondjees* or teachers. Some four hundred little Arab boys attend this school and squatted on the floor go through a course of Arabic grammar and the all-embracing Koran and the *hadis* or traditions. No other teaching is lawful. The golden rule, enunciated by Omar, though considered one of the false pearls of history, no doubt still holds good,—for all human needs the *Kalam-Ullah* or the Koran is all-sufficing, anything outside it must be consigned to the flames. On inquiry I was told no sort of outdoor games or athletics are encouraged. I recommended the introduction of cricket and lawn tennis, but our Arab mentor, who was personally conducting us, smiling shook his dubious head. One would think an Arab youngster with a flying ball, a skying kite and a trundling hoop would be all the better morally as well as physically, but the Arab elders evidently look on such a change as heretical. I fancy, however, if Koweyt is to march with the times, much of all these too stereotyped, old-world ways and methods of mental training will have to undergo a thorough and drastic change in the near future. The schoolmaster will have to be much abroad in these too long sun-dried lands of Ismail's descendants that have lain derelicts for ages.

CHAPTER XXXVIII.

We Visit our Host's House.

Passing on through a multitude of puzzling lanes and by-lanes flanked by bare, blank whited walls of the low, flat-roofed houses, with just rare ill-fitting doors and no windows opening on the street, we got to Dr. Kelly's house, and taking him along with us, we went on to pay our respects to the Political Agent, but found him away; so tramping on again through what seemed interminable zigzaging streets, we were glad to reach Mr. Abdul Latif's residence in what doubtless is a quarter where the well-to-do Koweytans reside, the Fauberg St. Germain of Koweyt. The house is very much the same as most Arab houses; the outside nothing to look at, but the interior was compact and comfortable, built square about an inner court yard. Our host is a swell in his way and likes to be up-to-date. He has a drawing-room furnished in English fashion, with cushioned sofas and easy chairs, tables, photo-albums, indifferent pictures, and some rather cheap ornaments. Here was seen even that modern monstrousity a gramophone, which to our immense delectation unwound some very tinkling Arab melodies. There were some small carpets here which are really saddle-bags, called 'khorgin,' but they made very handsome covers for chair-backs like ante-maccassers. These were of a very rich and beautiful pattern with incalculable number of stitches to a square inch. The more the stitches the better the make, that is the test. After a welcome rest and a wash, we

A modern Arab breakfast. went to breakfast in an adjoining room. It was strictly a *dèjeuner à la fourchette à l'Europeane*. Table and chairs, table-napery, plates and dishes, glasses, knives, forks and spoons all complete. Everything quite spick and span. Most of these articles were evidently brand new and used for the very first time in our honour and on our special behoof. Our good host was clearly proud of the elegant display. The food too though plentiful was rather an ineffectual attempt at English cookery. The Birmingham knives were so absolutely new, that they refused to operate on the *rôti* which consisted of a pair of large roast fowls; luckily there was no gravy served, else in the process of dissection there would have been a gravyous mishap or two. Our host's son and hopeful, a bright, handsome little chap in complete Arab costume, *akkal*, or hair-coil and all, who sat by his father, wisely avoided the European table implements, used his fingers freely and picked his share of the *morghi* clean, making a more satisfying meal than I fancy the rest of us did. Tea, in the form of a curious amalgam of some sort of tea and spices was served in large tea-cups with saucers ready combined with milk and generous contribution of sugar. We imbibed it without making a wry face, a difficult process of politeness, and this completed the morning meal.

The fashion of using furniture of all sorts of European style is evidently taking apace in these petty sheikh-doms on and about the Gulf, and any gentleman from and about the region of the Bombay Chukla-Bazaar who taking time by the forelock starts business here and hereabouts is bound to find his enterprise largely remunerative; but he must take the tide at the flood, or others will outstep him.

<small>The fashion in furniture.</small>

CHAPTER XXXIX.

Our Visit to the Sheik of Koweyt.

After having sent word ahead that we were coming, we were out again on the tramp and found our way to the Sheik's palace, a very rambling sort of building composed of several blocks, covering a wide area of ground. If not a commanding structure, it is certainly picturesque and possibly is roomy and comfortable, whilst from its many verandahs, and roof-terraces very lovely and far-spreading panoramic views are to be had all around. Mounting a bare and somewhat fragile wooden staircase, entirely out of keeping with a royal residence, we entered a large anteroom which flanks the Chief's council-hall and living-rooms. It was crowded with a heterogeneous lot of the Chief's retainers and body-guards 'with a swashing and martial outside' who eyed us askance and looked very bellicose and formidable, armed with a most artistic variety of guns, matchlocks, muskets, pistols of sorts, swords long, sabres curved, cut-throat knives, dirks and poniards, javelins and lances, enough to stock a small arsenal or make the fortune of a stage-manager who has mounted an oriental battle-piece. Clad in long flowing *burnoos, abba* or cloaks, white, black, brown striped or many coloured, with the head-kerchiefs dropping over the shoulders, wound round with white cord, or camel-hair *akkal,* these military gentry looked fierce, forbidding and fit for any martial stratagems, spoils or murderous exploit. Some stood at attention, others sat or reclined on the floor, chatting, smoking, dozing as they listed. Such-like one can imagine, must have been the wild cavaliers, who following the Amir Salar-ud-deen, foiled and beat back the repeated waves of the holy crusaders, or the fateful mandate-bearers of Hussain Sabah, whose name once carried

The Sheik's Bodyguard.

such terror over all Persia, Syria and Palestine. Making our way through these specimens of Arab soldiery, who gave us a good stare, we were ushered into the Council chamber, where our friend, Mr. Abdul Latif, presented us to the Ruler of Koweyt. The chamber where the Sheik deliberates on business of State with his councillors, is a large and spacious hall, with a lofty ceiling which is curiously ornamented with cheap, coloured prints of celebrated beauties glazed and set in small square gilt frames. At the head of the room which overlooks the harbour is a raised dais on which is a large gilt chair and the sides of the hall are lined with a number of sofas and chairs, the floor being richly carpetted. On the wall over the entrance hung a rather tawdry portrait in colours of H. M. the King-Emperor George V.

The Council Chamber of the Sheik.

The Sheik or Ruler of Koweyt, who is a K.C.I.E., seated in his state-chair on the dais, received us with much courtesy; standing up and shaking hands with us he made us sit on his left-hand quite close to the dais. He is a well-preserved, fine looking man of about 50 or a little over, with rather a sad, but highly intelligent countenance. He spoke neither English nor Hindustani, so that our equipment for conversation was of rather a halting character. The hall was full of the State councillors, mostly 'grave, reverend and potent' elderly men. One of these, who has visited Bombay, spoke Hindustani approximately, so that with his aid and that of Abdul Latif as our *tarjuman*, we held the usual brief coloquy with His Highness about our journey, our good health, about the weather and about some other casual topics. The Sheik said he means to visit Bombay soon and we of course volunteered our services to make him comfortable. Coffee was served and we took our leave.†

The Sheik of Koweyt.

Koweyt evidently means to keep abreast of the march of the times,

---

† The Sheik whom we met, died shortly after our visit, and the present Sheik is the brother of the deceased.

Progress in Koweyt.

as fast as could well be expected considering the centuries of customs, habits, traditions and fanatic convictions. In the palace and the customs' house electric light is already installed. How the Arabs must have gaped at first sight of it, ascribing it doubtless to Sheitan. The town has a water condenser, and it is likely there will be more of these very useful machines, seeing that the present water-supply is very defective, and drinking water has to be daily imported from Basra in boats fitted with tanks and distributed in the town in kerosene tins or sheep-skins costing an anna or its equivalent per tin or skin. The town also boasts of an ice-factory and one or two aerated-waters machines, the Arabs taking to these drinks like ducks to water.

The Sheik's motor-car.

Besides owning steam-launches, the Sheik sports a fine motor-car, which as it careers along, humping and snorting, his subjects have not yet ceased to regard as an inexplicable marvel or the uncanny offspring of some potent Jin or Afrit. The Sheik, it is reported, sent down one of his Arab retainers expressly to Bombay to be trained as a chauffeur. The man has returned an accomplished car-driver, and also, from all accounts, much given to liquor; so that when he is in his cups, the Sheik has for two or three days perforce to take to his horse or his donkey, or run the risk of a jolly smash up. The worthy chauffeur, without a rival at the time of our visit, was easily master of the situation. Wheeled carriages are not yet to be seen in Koweyt. If introduced now, I expect they would not be a success, unless and until the town possesses something other than the camel or donkey tracks that exist at present. It is highly probable that even before horse-carriages find their way to Koweyt, that great civiliser the railroad with its iron-horse is bound to be there, to give greatness and bring prosperity to this important port, standing at the mouth of the great sea-way, the Shat-el-Arab. Very cordially expressing our thanks to Mr. Abdul Latif, our very amiable host, for his friendly reception and courtesies, late in the afternoon we returned to the Zaiyanni, 'mighty pleased,' as Pepys would say, with our day's excursion.

CHAPTER XL.

The Basra Bar.

Leaving Koweyt harbour at 8 p. m. we steamed out some thirty miles passing between the large barren sand wastes of the Jazirat Bubyan on our left and the small island of Faelakkah on our right. At about 4 a. m. we anchored at the entrance of the troublesome Basra bar, awaiting high-tide.

The Basra Bar. This shallow piece of sea-water at the head of the Gulf is a troublesome obstacle in the way of steamers of a larger draught than the Zaiyanni. It is formed by the great estuary or delta of the combined *khors* or outlets of the Shat'-el-Arab, the Bamisher, the Joban, the Musa, the Abdullah and the Khalka, all which rivers, the largest being the Shat', flow down or through Persian Arabistan and Suziana into the Gulf. The Shat' forms the Western boundary of these countries. For countless ages all the silt, detritus and every description of fluvial deposits have been drained and washed down by these rivers to heap up and form the bed of the sea in this place, creating an ever-increasing barrier to sea-going vessels of even moderately heavy tonnage. Ships of over 3,000 tons burden, with full load, have thus their work cut out for them to negociate the Basra bar, both on entering it and clearing out of it without touching bottom or being badly stranded on the accumulated mud of all Mesopotamia and its adjoining provinces which here keeps silting up the bottom of the sea. The precise and propitious moment for crossing the bar is the height of the day-tide, and careful calculation on the part of the master of the ship is needed to be at the mouth of the Shat' at the correct nick of time. Early on the morning of the 23rd December when,

'Like a lobster boiled, the morn
From black to red began to turn,'

the Zaiyanni weighed anchor, and found herself in company with seven other steamers, at the sea-end of the bar. We could have taken the lead, but just missed doing so, as owing to the inexperience of our pilot, a young Persian, the ship grounded and it looked as if we were to be stuck there for another twelve hours, but our skipper having skilfully managed to extricate her just in time, and the tide yet serving, we were able to cross the Bar in the wake of the other seven steamers.

Crossing the Bar.

I was on the Bridge all the time and the eight steamers following one another in Indian file over the turbid waters was a most interesting sight. It was something like a naval review in a small way. The delta over the bar is broad enough, showing plenty of searoom, but the entrance into the mouth of the Shaṭ is by a narrow channel marked down by long lines of black buoys with just space between for a single ship to pass and that too at slow speed and at regulated intervals. Further on we had to pass over another portion of silted sea-bottom, forming a second or the Fao bar, which however is not so troublesome as the other obstructor we had just cleared.

How we pass the Basra Bar.

The British Government, now lord of Basra and all its territories, with its usual benign energy has started dredging operations to mitigate the troubles caused by these obstructive and dangerous impediments; but it's a case of *quieta non movere*, for from all accounts the work is so perfunctorily done that the cure is likely to be worse than the disease. Those in the know complain that this dredging is only shifting the body of the silt that causes all the trouble, extends it unevenly and renders it hummocky, whilst the surface of it which is dredged up, instead of being carried some twenty miles or more out to sea, is just deposited at a short distance away only to be rolled in again by strong tidal action making the mischief more trying than before.

Dredging the Bar.

CHAPTER XLI.

The Shatṭ-el-Arab.

As soon as the bar is crossed we enter the grand and broad flowing Shaṭ-el-Arab—or the river of the Arabs. Shatṭ means a river in Arabic, such as the Shatṭ-el-Hai, Shatṭ-el-Dialla, the Shatṭ-el-Adheim; but the Shatṭ-el-Arab is *the* Shatṭ, or *the* River *par excellence.* It is the broadest and the most important of the several rivers that drain Mesopotamia, flowing into and forming the great delta at the head of the Persian Gulf. Flowing southwards to the sea it commences its long course at Kurnah, where takes place the great meeting of the waters of the Euphrates, which is the Phrat or 'far flowing' of the Arabs, and the Tigris or 'swift flowing' like a '*tir*' or arrow. These rivers, taking their rise far away in the North amidst the perennial snows of the mountains of Armenia and swollen with their numerous tributaries, united become the grand Shatṭ-el-Arab, which thus connects the ancient and classic land of Mesopotamia—'that blessed word' (or is it the reverse?) now so much on the tongues of men—with the Persian Gulf. Here once flourished the mighty empires of Assyria, Babylonia, Media, Persia and Parthia. This famous land between the twain rivers, where once flourished these five great monarchies, has lain 'a derelict for over two thousand years,' specially after the terrible tornados that swept over it under the Eastern Huns and the Mongols, who destroyed the first great Caliphate and its splendid civilization, leaving behind them dearth and desolation. Everywhere the Turks who came in later did little to revive the ancient glory and prosperity of the land. Happily it has now become British by force of arms and through the incurable folly of its late possessors. It is the general opinion that it

<small>The great River.</small>

<small>Mesopotamia.</small>

would be an unaccountable folly if Great Britain ever parts with it; that, in fact—

> 'The good old rule, the simple plan
> That they shall take who have the power,
> And they shall keep who can,'

shall prevail and '*Mesopot,*' as the soldier has baptised it with his blood, should not be deprived of the chance it has now got, the chance that the *pax Britannica* offers it, of once more being a land of plenty, prosperous and free. Experts say that its possibilities are such as to make it a veritable Eldorado such as will go far to recoup more than half the costs of this War; that under a sane, honest, capable and enterprising administration such as is possible and now available under British-Indian rule the country is bound to flourish immensely in various ways and particularly as a grain (wheat specially) and cotton-growing country. During the Roman world-rule 'Mesopot' was one of the great granaries of Europe. It could easily become such again with proper irrigation and facile communication by land and water, and these essentials are of easy attainment with the complete control of the railways and the Euphrates, the Tigris and their great adjunct the Shat'-el-Arab in British hands. These advantages, aided and made the best of by British and Indian pluck, energy, skill and enterprise, promise and assure a great future for this ancient land of the great rivers. 'It awaits only the *open sesame*' (as Mr. Hubbard puts it in his work just out 'From the Gulf to Ararat,') 'of the modern irrigation engineer to unlock its portals and supply food for half a continent.' The more important towns in Eastern Asiatic Turkey such as Mosul, Diarbeker, Samara and Baghdad stand on the banks of the Tigris. These three great rivers, the historic waterways of commerce in ancient times between Europe and all Asia, find frequent mention in Arab and Persian literature, with reference especially to their size and pre-eminence. Maulana Jallal-ud-deen Rumi, the great Sufi poet and mystic, writes of them in his extraordinary poem the *Mathnavi*—

'*Ai ye ké under chasmai-shur ast jat,*
Tu ché dani Shat,? O Jeihun, O Phrat?'
'O ye! who 'mong salt springs have your habitat,
What can ye know of the Shat?, the Jeihun and Phrat?'

The Shat? gathering the waters of the Jeihun and the Phrat that form and bound Mesopotamia, becomes a noble river a good thousand yards wide at its commencement at Kornah, makes its way down to the South in an ample and stately flood, flowing straight into the Gulf by a single embouchure, where it is a mile and more in width. It is a tidal river flowing between high banks much of its way and is navigable the whole length of its course for sea-going steamers of considerable burden as far as Basra and further up for river boats. Great and valuable as the Shat? is for commercial and strategic purposes, it is singular that between Fao and Kornah, except Mahomerah and of course Basra, there are no great towns situated on it.

Kornah, the reputed site of the garden of Eden, at its head, it is worth noting, struck Sir John Malcolm when in this neighbourhood, as a most important place from a military point of view and with a prescient eye he recommended the Marquess of Wellesley, then Governor-General of India, to obtain or take and annex, for he considered that commanding as the place does the junction of the three rivers it could be so fortified as to be made inexpugnable so as it could keep in wholesome check all the turbulent and treacherous Arab and other tribes and peoples that inhabit or range over these regions and could exercise a most salutary and exacting influence over all the wild countries bordering on these rivers from Baghdad to Bassora. Little could the great fighting Governor-General have anticipated a time, a hundred years after him, when the British-Indian forces would be having all their work cut out for them, victoriously fighting their way up mile by mile in among the inhospitable swamps of the Tigris with Kornah, captured and held, as one of their important military bases.

The value of Kornah.

On the Banks of the Shaṭ. The banks of the Shaṭ-el-Arab are studded with small Arab villages or nomad settlements, composed of a cluster of huts made of the large reeds that fringe the riverside. The huts are lightly built with date-tree trunks and stocks for supports and thatched with reeds. Sometimes when the nomads shift their ground the huts are turned to rafts. Many of these settlements are just small farms where sheep, cattle and poultry are reared and I saw numerous flocks of domestic ducks, geese and fowls about the creeks by which these places are approached.

Wild game birds. Wild ducks in great variety, snipe, sand-grouse and other water fowls and game birds affording good *shikar* abound in these localities, where the reeds and marsh bulrushes provide them with good nesting and feeding ground. I saw several flocks of wild ducks floating unscared and unconcerned quite within sight of our moving steamer.

The buffalo. Here too, since leaving Bombay, I saw again the ungainly buffalo, the Persian species not differing observably from the Indian animal. At this season of the year I saw very few cows or bullocks and the horse too seemed to be scarce about here. It was again after many days that on the Shaṭ I saw kites and eagles, which flew in numbers above the stationary steamers, watching for flotsam and jetsam that might come their way and now and then swooping in among the screaming gulls and scaring them. I noticed that these regions about the great Arab river are happy in the absence of that sable iniquity we know in Bombay, that winged pest and marauder the black and gray-necked crow. In his place, however Basra has a beautiful bird of its own no doubt a cousin-german of the other, though not in any great number.

The white crow. This is the fine large white crow, with head and body of a dull white and raven wings. I saw only a few of these among the date-trees and to outward appearance they seemed to be quite respectable members of the tribe. Big game is not found anywhere near the banks of the Shaṭ, but foxes, jackals and wild pigs might help to make a bag for an intrepid shikari.

CHAPTER XLII.

The Land of the Date.

I have entitled this little volume 'The Land of the Date.' I have so far described the places visited on the Gulf, it is time now having entered the Vilayet or province of Basra, to give some account of these vast date-producing areas bordering on both banks of the great Shat'-el-Arab, as well as of the fruit for which the land is famous. Here on the Shat' we are in the true native land of the date. Though the date-palm flourishes more or less luxuriantly all along the Gulf coast from far below Bahrein to Koweyt, it is, here, on entering this broad river, that we are in the true home of the date tree. Here it is native of the soil, and the excellence of its fruit is largely due, I should say, to the fertilising waters of the river on both banks of which for miles inland to East and West of it, are to be seen the thickly planted forests of this wonderful tree. The word date has an instructive derivation. It comes from the Greek *dactylos*, a finger, the shape of the fruit, having something of the appearance of the human digit, and thus the botanical name of the tree *Phœnix dactylifera*, or the Phœnician finger-bearer, takes us far back to hoary antiquity when the early settlers from Phœnicia on the Gulf repatriated themselves and carried the date-tree with them to the Eastern, as well as possibly the Southern or African shores of the Mediterranean. In the plains of Basra, which the Shat' bisects, not a hill is in sight; whichever way you turn the land is level and the landscape is bounded by date-trees; nothing but date-trees,—green, graceful, refreshing. The Arab dwellers of these lands devote their most careful attention to their cultivation. Prolific as these trees are here their fructification owing

<small>The word Date.</small>

<small>The cultivation of the date tree.</small>

to the absence of bees has to be increased by the cutting away of the pollen-laden spathes of the male tree at given seasons and through the meshes of a coarse bag dusting the female flowers with the same; at the same time the trees are fed with a manure obtained from the ray fish, called *awwal,* putrified by being steeped in water, a treatment which is found very stimulating. Though the flora of the Shat' country includes the mulberry, the grape-vine and fig, chiefly cultivated in private gardens, also tamarind-trees, the *tamar-i-hind* or the Hindustani date as the Arabs and Persians call our common culinary relish, and even some dwarfish *ber-*trees (the Indian jujube) so familiar in the Bombay Presidency and in other parts of India; it is the date-tree that is pre-eminently the fruit-tree of these regions and without a rival in the estimation of the people. Standing on the steamer's deck as we go up or down stream, you see nothing but endless tracts crowded with the ever-verdant, feathery foliage of the delightsome date-palm. Hardly any other palm is cultivated where it flourishes, for it is a curious fact, so far as I have observed, that these lands where it grows so abundantly and to such perfection, no other variety of the genus palm is to be seen. All along the Gulf, or about the Shat' I saw no cocoanut-palm, nor the areca palm, nor the talipot-palm, nor the Khandala-palm, nor the bottle-palm, nor the fan-shaped traveller's palm, nor the sago-palm, nor any of the other varieties so commonly found in India and the islands of the Indian Seas. The date-trees evidently suffice for all the Arab's wants; the date-groves are the granary, the treasury, the mint so to say, of the peoples of these parts of Arabia. The date has well been christened by an early traveller, as 'the bread of the land, the staff of life, and the staple of commerce,' of the Arabs all about the Gulf and the Shat'. It has been and is unmistakably the main source of the sustenance of the poor and the wealth of the rich of this country. Something in the style of the fifth Commandment and rightly has the Mussalman Prophet commanded, 'Honour the date-

The flora of the Shat' country.

Absence of other palms.

The value of the date-tree.

tree for she is your mother.' To eat dates the first thing in the morning on breaking your fast is considered an act of piety as the Arab proverb hath it, '*ham khoorma, ham sawab,*'—that is, to eat dates and to do a good deed has the same merit.

CHAPTER XLIII.

Date Cultivation.

As the lotus is the symbol of India, the olive that of Syria, the rose-tree that of England, the date-palm is the symbol of Arabia and particularly of this part where flows the stately Shat̕. The Arab land-owners and their hinds or servants, the poorer villagers, all treat it with the greatest respect and care and are its skilful if somewhat primitive cultivators. The grove-lands are hollowed out and divided into squares or oblongs by embankments, something like our paddyfields in India. Within these are planted the trees in regular, measured rows. The Shat̕ has all along its banks numerous creeks that run inland a considerable way navigable for small boats and about which stand the riparian villages. These river-inlets serve indifferently 'as laundries, bath-rooms and drains for the inhabitants.' At low-tide they emit a powerful odour that is far from refreshing, but at high-tide they are filled with the river water, which is then diverted into the plantations by sluices which are opened or banked up with earth as needed and the trees are in this way regularly irrigated and grow up and remain robust and fruitful. These trees are largely divided into two kinds, the short and the tall trees, but all are uniformly larger and stouter in the girth than those we have in several parts of India, where the fruit never comes to perfection. The cultivation of the date-palm is the chief agriculture and the main business concern of the Arabs' life in these parts. The tree along the Shat̕ is singularly fructiferous and the excellent quality of its fruit, so renowned all over the world, must I think be accounted for by the peculiar moist heat of the Shat̕ or Basra country during April, May, June, July and August. The heat then is intense and has been described as infernal—but it is needful

The creeks of the Shat̕.

and favourable to the full growth and perfection of the fruit, which ripens in August and September, when comes the season of the date harvest—the Arab's harvest home; people then go out on picnic parties to the palm groves and have a ripping time of it, enjoying the luciotrs fresh date amidst much rural amusement and rejoicing. The fruit eaten fresh, just as it fully ripens, is more dilicious, more juicy and more nutritious than the finest hot-house English grape. Great are the varieties of the date; but the dark-red variety is esteemed the best, whilst the long yellow or golden date seemingly having no stone gives the finest flavour and is esteemed a real dainty. The Arab housewife is skilled in preparing a great number of tasty dishes from the fruit cooked in different ways—green, dried, crushed, stewed or mingled with meat, fish or curds—they are eaten at the different seasons. From the date is also made a date syrup called *tummair* and much used for sweetening purposes. A date-palm shooting up fifty feet and more with its canopy of waving, bristle-pointed leaves, its spathe gemmed with thousands of blossoms and its fruit hanging in golden clusters, rivalling the apples of the Hesperides, is a lovely sight to behold; 'a vision of delight' indeed. The date-tree besides furnishing its abundant fruit so valuable as human food, affords materials for a score and more of domestic uses. It is thus well pronounced to be the most useful product of the vegetable kingdom. A veritable boon and blessing in these desert-bound lands of the date. Much of the fruit fails to ripen. This is termed '*salang*' and kneaded with dried fish is much eaten by the poorer classes. Mixed with ground date-stones, which too are thus put to use, and fish-bones the *salang* makes nutritive fodder for cattle, camels and asses. Even horses relish it. The pith of the green spathe again makes good eating, and distilled, it yields a sweet liquid the Arabs call *tara*, which is much used for making sherbet and might with due skill be turned into sugar. From this term *tara* we doubtless get our Indian word *tarri* and the English hybrid toddy. It also gives the word *tar* or *tad*,

The date harvest.

The date-palm a fine sight.

Its many uses.

the talipot palm of India and gives expression to Tadmor or Palmyra, the city of palms, which the noble Queen Zenobia rendered so famous and which now stands desolate and in ruins amidst the sands of Syria for the Cookist to gape at. Another use is the making of very serviceable ropes from the green fibres of the leaf-stocks whilst much of the fuel used in these parts so lacking in wood comes from the dried stocks; the pinnated leaves are turned into fans, mats, baskets and bedding, providing livelihood for the people. The whole leaves are also used as awning stretched overhead across the narrower ways of the bazaars affording shade and coolness. The trunks of the trees past-bearing fruit are commonly employed for shoring the banks of the creeks and rivers to prevent erosion or crumbling; also for extemporised bridges across the muddy creeks and foot-ways at the river-side landing-places. These trunks come useful too for the door-posts and cut in even strips for roof battens for the huts or sheds of the poor people. Cut into rounds you have stools and seats of a rough and ready sort, whilst sawn into halves and scooped out they do duty as water-carriers from grove to grove. We must not forget to mention another use of the all-providing date-tree and this is a curious sort of cot or *charpoy* very like a hen-coop and might be used as such for the nonce. These are made from the split leaf-stocks and are quite serviceable, being strong enough and easily portable. Again any group or grove of these beautiful trees affords the people shady walks and resting places, whilst since very early days of Eastern history the prince or judge would hold his levée or put up his judgment seat under its grateful branches. As is reported, Deborah, the heroine and prophetess, 'judged Israel under the palm-tree.' In these lands of the date by the Shat' and above and below it, the date-tree, proclaimed by the Prophet 'the mother of the Arabs,' does not as yet appear to be tapped for the liquor for which alone it is cultivated along the shores of Bombay. The Arab has not up to now learnt to extract this yet another useful product from his favourite tree, either as an

The Juice of the Date-palm.

exhilerating and pleasant beverage or for turning it into sugar as is done in some parts of India. But we live and learn and these uses of the date-palm, it may be presumed, are likely to follow definite British occupation, by way of social amelioration and a new industry. If, however, the Koranic injunction saves the people let us hope, from the temptation of too copiously indulging in this sacharine drink either fresh or fermented or distilled, such as maketh the heart of that good man the Parsee priest to rejoice and giveth him a cheerful countenance, there is nothing to prevent the juice of the palm being turned to good account in manufacturing it into sugar and so adding a very paying staple to the trade of the Shatt' and the Gulf countries.

Seeing how far and wide and extensive are the lands stretching away from the Shatt', it struck me that in skilful hands with proper foresight and energy there is room there enough and to spare for raising such valuable field-crops as rice and other cereals and sugar-cane where only the date-tree now reigns single and supreme, seeing how plentiful, constant and ready-at-hand is the water-supply from these great rivers. The soil is favourable and with scientific irrigation fertility is assured.

Cultivation of Rice and Sugar-cane.

CHAPTER XLIV.

Approaching Mohomerah.

About 18 miles northward from the outer buoy where we enter the Basra bar, we pass the little town or hamlet of Fao, a very barren, desolate spot, all sand and marsh, on the right bank of the Shat', chiefly important at present for its telegraph and wireless signalling stations which connect the British-Indian and Turkish lines or systems of telegraphs *via* Bushire. Here a sort of a battle was fought with the Turks previous to the fall of Basra. Fao is used also as an advanced guard-post for inspection and control of shipping that here enter the Shat'. It is the threshold of Mesopotamia. Some years back the Turks constructed a fort here, causing considerable flutter and excitement in the political dovecotes; but no guns were ever mounted probably owing to the more immediate needs of the Turkish officials, the money meant for munitions being diverted to their own pockets and no questions asked. This fort has been practically abandoned. Foreign up-going steamers have to halt here awaiting permit to proceed higher up; accordingly several of them that had crossed the Bar in front of us were detained here and the Zaiyanni was able to forge on ahead of them.

<small>Fao</small>

When the war is victoriously over and the British-Indian grip over the entire Shat'-el-Arab and its great fluvial feeders is firmly fixed, Fao, now a sleepy hollow of the sleepiest and a howling wilderness to boot, might be turned into a bright and blooming watering-place close to the sea to which the people of Basra, Abadan, Mohomerah, Kornah and from Baghdad way too could readily resort by rail or river for healthful change, pleasurable holiday, inspiring week-ends, and (for the native gentry) a good

<small>Future of Fao.</small>

periodical much needed wash-up and ablution in the salt-sea waves. The place promises (provided the aforesaid grip is no way relaxed) to become a favourite recreation ground during the cold season and if people are wide awake they might do worse than get about and invest in land, now to be had for the asking, in this neighbourhood.

At Fao is the real entrance into the main stream of the Shat'. On the opposite or Persian side is the fantastically shaped large island of Abadan formed by the Shat' on the one side and the zigzag course of the river Bhameshir on the other, and extending as far up as Mohomerah, forty miles to the North. Here too begin the primeval evergreen groves or rather forests of date-trees that crowd and cluster and flourish over both banks of the River far beyond Basra. Several miles up the river, steaming slowly, we passed the town of Abadan on its left bank. It is entirely a modern town, owing its rise to the Anglo-Persian Oil Co. of which it is the head quarters. This new-born corner of the far-flung British Empire proclaims its *raison d'être* from afar by the breeze that wafted the fragrance of 'the oyle stynking horryblye,' as old Joseph Barbaro hath it when referring to Baku. The oil wells or diggings are situated some 150 miles away at Ahwaz to the North-East on the Karun river whence pipes in a straight line convey the precious petroleum to Abadan, where it is shipped in specially constructed tank-steamers suited to shallow river traffic and carried on to Basra and higher up on the one hand to meet the present military demand for it, and on the other hand for export to other countries over the Bar where the oil has to be transhipped into the large oil steamers that are unable to negociate the Bar.

<small>We enter the Shat'.</small>

<small>Abadan and its rock oil.</small>

At the commencement of the present Mesopotamian campaign great trouble and anxiety was experienced for the safety of these oil-wells, the capture or destruction of which was planned and instantly threatened by the German intriguers in Persia backed as they were by many Persians in power, whom the Boche had cajoled, frighted or bribed into

<small>Safety of the oil wells.</small>

compliance. The precious wells were however saved and just in time by the prompt action of the British Government by General Gorringe's expedition up the Karun and are now safe-guarded effectively by the suppression of all tribal disorders in their neighbourhood and by the stationing at Ahwaz of a sufficient field-force. Ahwaz thus becomes a far away British outpost in Persian territory doing very valuable service at the present juncture. Abadan presents an extraordinarily interesting sight with its many lines of capacious oil-tanks its factories with tall chimneys belching black smoke, its numerous resounding, busy work-shops, its well-laid-out residences, and its busy wharfs and shipping-yards that line its river-front, where are laid a number of narrow tram-lines connected with the oil-tanks, and on which ply constantly miniature trains drawn by puffing little toylike, miniature locomotives. Abadan is thus, as may be conceived, a busy, lively grimy stink-producing ever-growing manufacturing town, curiously and strikingly in contrast with all its surroundings. It is within hail almost of the ruins of the palaces of Persepolis and Suza, where lived, and gloried Darius and Xerces and Arta-Xerces, kings of kings and where the great Macedonian triumphed and held high revels. Springing up in a few years, as if by some enchanter's command in a land that has remained stationary, barren and lifeless as it were, for over thirty centuries; in a land which witnessed the rise, the glory, the overthrow and the ruins of mighty empires that have passed away, leaving but sand-blown mounds and wonder-moving sculptures bruised and overthrown in 'colossal wreck,' as epitaphs of the might, the pomp and glory and the greatness that are no more, decayed, lost and buried in the oblivion of Time. 'Ichabod' has long been writ large over this ancient land of which Khayyam moralises:—

Appearance of Abadan.

'Thy drums are hushed, thy 'larums have rung truce.'

But the world around is waking into vivid life again and Abadan happily points out this change. For it is indeed springing up into a busy hive of men, peopling the desert sands. It is the first modern manufacturing town I believe in all these Asiatic regions and promises to become a great cradle of industry; a sort of second Baku in fact and being within easy hail of India, it is for us all the more interesting and important.

CHAPTER XLV.

Mohomerah and the Karun River.

Arrival at Mohomerah.

Twelve miles further up the Shat' we reached Mohomerah, a Persian town, capital of Persian Arabistan and anchored there at 2 p. m. B. I. S. S. Dumra with the Bombay mails had got in there just before us and was at anchor in front of us; but as it stayed only to deliver mails, and cleared away soon after our arrival, the Zaiyanni shifted her mooring and took up the more convenient berth which the Dumra vacated, being nearer to the town. Dr. Lincoln, the Consulate Medical Officer, with Mirza Mohomed Hussein, the Secretary to the Agent of the P. G. N. Company, came aboard. I found them both very agreeable people and a good part of the afternoon was spent with them over tea and cakes and exchange of news. After 18 days of sea with nought but barren hills and desert-coasts in view, the river scenery was a welcome variation, with its miles and miles of waving date-palms and with the constant passing up and down of ships and steamers and old-world country-craft of all sorts and sizes on the broad agate-greenish waters of the noble Shat'. Soon after sun-down a heavy, white mist or fog arose and quite obscured both banks. Mohomerah stands on the site of what once was the ancient town of Bahmishir or Bahman-Ardesir, the name and memory of which is still preserved in the considerable river Bahmishir, which making a sluggish and circuitous course to the East of the island of Abadan flows South into the Persian Gulf. The modern town with a population of about 10,000 souls, is situated on the right bank of the Hafar, where the waters of the Karun, deviated from its natural channel, flow westward into the Shat', close to where the Zaiyanni stood anchored. It is a very pretty spot.

Site of Mohomerah.

The Karun River. The Karun, or *Kuhrang* (hill-coloured) river rises in the Zardeh-Kuh range to the North of the town of Ahwaz and after a troublous and torturous course, intercepted by rapids and often in floods, descending through the turbulent country of the Bakhtiaris, passing by the towns of Shuster and Ahwaz, it finds its waters before reaching the Bahmisher, which is its natural channel, largely deflected by the Hafar into the Shat'. It was formerly known as the Pasi-tigris or the lesser Tigris and Alexander the Great on his way back from India to Suza had thrown across it a bridge of boats.

The Hafar. The Hafar is a broad waterway about three or four miles long, and connects the Karun with the Shat'. The word Hafar in Arabic signifies a canal, digging or ditch and points to its artificial construction. It was dug out about A.C. 980 in order to bring Ahwaz other inland Persian towns into closer and more direct communication with Basra, making Mohomerah the river-port of Persia.

Town of Ahwaz. Since 1889, Mohomerah, at the junction of the Hafar and the Shat', has risen into greater importance owing to the opening of international navigation as far as the rapids of the Karun near Ahwaz, some hundred and seventeen miles away. Ahwaz too is rising into importance both on account of the oil-wells it commands and of its being the trade centre for the interior of this part of Persia. The scheme of a railway from Ahwaz into the interior held up by the war, if it comes to completion would give it still greater importance, when in the words of Lord Curzon, 'the inhabitants will be drawn into the mesh of the Lancashire cotton-spinner and the Hindu artizan.' Its climate is said to be agreeable and salubrious. The river-way, though longer than going overland, is much safer and more convenient both for transit of goods and passengers, owing to a well-managed service of river-steamers which exists between Ahwaz and Mohomerah, and joining the caravan routes into the interior above Shuster, it opens the shortest land route to Isphahan the old capital of Shah Abbas, which its citizens fondly call '*Isphahan nisf-i-Jehan*,' that is, Isphahan is half the world, and from there into the considerable commercially important districts of Persia.

CHAPTER XLVI.

Town of Mohomerah.

Christmas Day we spent at Mohomerah, seeing such sights as the town affords. After an early breakfast in state with the Captain and all his officers assembled in the dining saloon, which was prettily decorated, the Captain, the Chief Engineer and I, taking a *bellam*, were rowed round the bend where the Karun-cum-Hafar joins the Shat' and where on the left hand, flush with the water, stands Mohomerah amidst very pretty surroundings, stretching up the Hafar a considerable way. Just at this corner is the Customs House, as busy as any place or person could be said to be busy in Persia; next to it stands the British Vice-Consulate easily distinguishable by the flag staff surmounted by the familiar flag. On the banks just opposite is the doctor's house, the hospital, the forlorn-looking quarantine station, a few other houses and some boat-building yards rich in mud. On a line with the Consulate are various offices and among these in a garden of rose trees and grape-vines stands a large upper-storied house which is the office of P. G. N. Co.'s Agent. Here we landed on Persian soil once more, stepping over a tremulous slippery plank, which spanned the muddy strand from boat to the landing-steps. The Agent, Hajee Mohomed Mushiri, Rais-at-Tajarat,

<small>Hajee Mushiri the ship's agent.</small> the principal minister of the Sheikh, a very dignified Persian gentleman seated or rather squatted at his low desk, received us with great civility and the conventional inquiries. As the old gentleman looked asthmatic and complained of being troubled with lumbago, the office-room was hermetically closed up and though pretty large was feeling decidedly stuffy. It was sumptuously-carpeted, and was furnished

with some pretty articles such as carved Indian and Chinese tables, chairs and shelves, some pretty crockery, mirrors and several very tawdry prints and pictures and indifferent, faded photographs. Among these virtuosities it was a bit of a surprise to find an elegant miniature church-organ, with many pipes and stops. I wondered what use it could ever be put to by the owner or by the sort of gentry, a varied assortment of Arab and Persian sailors and landsmen, who were in and out of the office. Whilst we sat there the son and heir of the Sheik of Mohomerah dropped in and we were introduced to him by the Rais. Our ceremonious visit was brought to a close by the serving of hot tea in little glasses—'made in Germany'—without milk, but sweetened with a too bounteous tablespoon. Having courteously swallowed a glassful each of this peculiarly Persian mixture, and not relishing a repetition of the dose, we took our departure. The Agents' Secretary, the Mirza Mohomed Hussein was there and made himself very friendly. He was educated in Bombay spoke English with fluency and a perfect accent. A man of the world evidently, thoroughly well informed *jusquaux bouts des ongles* in the history and affairs of Persia and her neighbours, a handsome figure and charming manners, he struck me as one who would make an ideal travelling companion, if one were wanted for a leisurely tramp in the land of the Shahs. Whilst the Captain remained to transact business, the Engineer and I, furnished with a guide by the Mirza, we made a prolonged round of the bazaars of this town, which extend a good way along the canal front, intersect some muddy creeks and are over half a mile deep. There was nothing to distinguish them from others I have described. There are the same lanes and alleys crossing each other, the same sort of shops and stalls, the same miscellaneous crowds with the same composite jabber of tongues, the same sort of goods and commodities with nothing of local make to strike a stranger's eye, the same footways, the same squalor and absence of

The Mirza M. Hussein.

Mohomerah Bazaars.

Smells, assortment of. sanitation and the same more or less pungent and overpowering odours such as a sensitive nostril could distinctly enumerate as Coleridge did of Cologne, the ill-drained creeks contributing considerably thereto. To these aboriginal perfumes that here assail one's nose, a new specimen has been added since the oil-works have been started at Abadan. For the two nights we lay at anchor on the river abreast of Mohomerah we felt the fragrance of petroleum wafted over by the slightest breeze that blew from the warm South. It was a case something different rather to what the poet sings of:—

> 'The sweet South
> That breathes upon banks of violets
> Stealing and giving odour.'

This oil-laden zephyr though said to be salubrious as a disinfectant was not pleasant and my bottle of smelling salts with a dash in it of eucalyptus came in very useful. Given the delightful and balmy winter weather we were experiencing and for a few vacation-days, Mohomerah is a pleasant enough place to linger in, making excursions to Ahwaz and Shuster which is classic soil and archæologically most interesting, but for the greater part of the year one would I should say, much prefer to live well out of it.

View over the Hafar. Returning to the office, we took boat again and were rowed some way up the Hafar or canal alongside of the town and down again by the opposite bank. Both sides are covered with endless, thickly planted groves of date-trees, and the town with its white houses in the midst of gardens, in a background of palms, its front crowded with boats at anchor or plying up or down, presented a very pretty sight as we saw it across the water.

Water temperature. A curious thing to be remarked here is the difference of temperature observed throughout the year, between the waters of the Shaṭ and those of the Karun-cum-Hafar right up to the line where they mingle. The latter are always distinctly cooler or colder.

After our very interesting visit ashore we got back to the Zaiyanni for late tea and very welcome rest.

Mohomerah history. Formerly Mohomerah nominally governed by an Arab Sheik, was alternately in Turkish and in Persian hands owing to interminable squabbles over the respective frontiers which each side delimited as best suited them, till in 1847, after years of worrying and costly preliminaries, a commission of British, Russian, Turkish and Persian officers and officials settled the business and definitely demarkating the boundaries, assigned Mohomerah to the Persians. Since then it has been the seat of a Persian Governor, who at present is the Sheikh Khazal.

The Sheikh of Mohomerah. He is a K. C. I. E. and also a K. C. S. I. and the chief of the important Ka'ab Arabs who immigrated to these parts some 250 years ago, renouncing the Sultan's rule and preferring the Shah's. The Chief is practically the independent ruler of the province of Arabistan, subject to the more or less nominal control of the Shah's *Karguzar* or resident-agent. Among his other dignities, he is entitled to a salute from all steamers passing up to Basra, in recognition of useful help rendered by him or his father, I am not clear which, to an English vessel attacked here-abouts by pirates some years ago, when piracy was not infrequent on the Shatt. During the short Persian war in 1857 Mohomerah was taken by the British and held till the conclusion of Peace.

CHAPTER XLVII.

Approaching Al Basorah or Basra.

Basra is twenty-six miles from Mohomerah. Weighing anchor at 9 a. m. we left the latter place and proceeded on the final and most interesting stage of our voyage. We were now in the land of the date. The noble Shat, here narrows considerably, being split up by the large island of Dabbah on our left, which covered with date palms, is evidently the result of ages of alluvial accretion. On our right we passed Falia, a large village where is built along the riverside the palace of the Mohomerah Sheik. Here we fired the customary salute by exploding a detonator, and it was punctiliously returned from two rusty cannons that stood on the river bank, half buried in mud. A party of slatternly soldiery, in some what ragged regimentals, doubtless the Governor's body-guard, were idly standing by to watch this honourable and rather risky display. The salute is looked upon as a great compliment and not to be lightly neglected on any account. Its omission would seriously offend the Sheikhal dignity, if not create a *casus belli*. This body-guard of negroes attends the Sheikh on all occasions wherever he goes, and does duty as very necessary life-guards in a quarter of the world where the taking of life is an act of high policy or commendable politics. The Sheikh's palace is an extensive building on the right as we go up with a rather imposing or showy gateway, having a heraldic lion standing on each post. It is the Sheik's favourite residence. Attached to it on one side is a large theatre-house, where the Chief frequently tries to dispel the monotony of life in such a dreary country by lavishly entertaining bands of gypsy and other dancing girls that roaming the land periodically find their

<small>We salute the Sheik or Governor of Mohomerah.</small>

<small>The Sheik's palace.</small>

way down here from Roumania and have a right good time of it. From all accounts it is something of a saturnalia. Then the fun is fast and furious; high and low, simple and sophisticated have a long bout of the rout and revelry and for the time being the quoranic teetotaller is on the strike if report and rumour be true. Close to it are the residences of his councillors. The palace fixes the boundary line between Persian territory and Turkish. A little further up we come against on our right a long and narrow island fringed with scrub and reeds, called Quarantine Island. Between the southern end of this and the northern end of the Dubbah island the river makes a bend so narrow that ordinarily even it is difficult to negotiate, especially if another steamer coming down suddenly shows itself from the opposite side. Yet it is just at this narrow channel of the river, as soon as Turkey declared or was dragged into war against the Allies, the resourceful Germans then controlling the Turkish forces in Mesopotamia, sank four steamers across in a line, one of these the Ecbatana, a large ship, and another is one which the Turks had rented and used as a light-ship. They of course intended thus effectively to block the river passage up to Basra. Luckily the fell design failed, for the rushing Shatt, the ebbing tide aiding it, swept aside the Ecbatana which had almost touched the Dabbah shore, and left fair-way enough for just one steamer to creep clear through at a time. When I passed by, the funnel of the head-boat and her two masts were still visible well above the water, and captains of steamers to and from Basra have still a trying time of it when passing through, the passage having to be manœuvred with care and always in daylight.

The Barrier of sunken ships.

Having turned this very awkward corner, we had our first view of Basra with its port of Ashaar which presented the picture of a fine oriental city, as we saw it from the ship's bridge, rising like Venice out of the circumambient waters, and surrounded by groves of crowding date-palms with their waving feathery branches. A long array of houses lined the

First sight of Basra.

right bank of the River, the waters of which for miles were crowded with shipping of all sorts, the many masts and funnels and flags of which adding to the picturesqueness of the scene.

The first house we sighted is the *Beyt-Nameh*, standing amidst a large garden of oleanders, orange-trees and trailing grape-vines, the property of an Arab or Turkish gentleman, commandeered and turned into an officers' hospital made comfortable with electric lighting, fans and hot and cold water laid on; the modern soldier is a costly article and needs much coddling. Soon after noon we glided to our anchorage in the wake of a long line of steamers moored higher up. We considered ourselves lucky in not being shunted more than two and half miles away from the Ashaar creek, which is the chief landing-place of Basra.

The Beyt-Nameh.

The winter is the rainy-season in these regions of the Shatt and her parents the Euphrates and Tigris and before getting into port here we encountered a duststorm, happily swept away by a smart shower of rain. The temperature was comfortably cold, rendered all the pleasanter by occasional little rain-drizzle.

The weather.

CHAPTER XLVIII.

The Town of Basra.

All Basora, as the Arabs call it, and nowadays commonly yclept Basra, stands midway on the right bank of the Shat'. Milton mentions it:—

'Suziana to Balsara's Haven.'

This famous town whence Sinbad's soul once and again so 'longed to sail the seas and see foreign countries and company with merchants and hear new things,' is now in British hands. It is the capital of the important vilayat of Basra (no longer Turkish) which contains the towns of Kornah, Amara, Kut-el-Amara, Nasarieh Sukes-Sheik and others, now first brought to the notice of the world by the victories of the British-Indian forces, whose triumphal progress up and along the three great rivers marks the permanent, let us hope, disappearance of the unspeakable Turk from these latitudes of Asia Minor. Basra is the great date-port of the world, the port or true commercial gate-way of the erstwhile City of the Caliphs, *Bagh-i-Dad*, 'the Flower-garden of Justice,' connecting it and the *Dar-el-khalifeh* with Greater Asia. It was founded by the Khaliph Omar in 635 A.C.

History of Basra.

The original city, on an ancient arm of the Euphrates, was situated some eight miles to the South-West of the modern city and the old site is still marked by considerable ruins awaiting exploration. Its prosperity declined with the power of the Abbasid Khaliphs, when the canals were neglected and communication with the Gulf cut off. Then arose the present Basra well on the banks of the Shatt-el-Arab, and owing to its favourable situation soon became famous as one of the most considerable cities of Arabia. Built on the western bank of the Shatt' it is seventy miles from the river's mouth. With its old walls, once seven miles in circumference, enclosing numerous gardens and date orchards, its five gates, its crowded caravanserais, its lively *kavakhanas*, its public baths, mosques and famous *madresahs*, its busy water-front whence Sinbad, the Menchausen of the East must have sailed on his wonderful voyages, Al Basorah must have been a fine oppulent and thriving city in the olden days of its glory. Its first connection with Bombay dates from 1639, when the E. I. Company ruling in Surat, sent two agents to establish a factory there. The trade intercourse however was not very brisk or promising till 1661, when a capitulation was signed between the Sublime Porte and Charles II, who, in the State paper that passed between them, is described (it is amusing to note) as 'the glorious among the Princes of Jesus, the reverenced of the people of the Messiah, ... Lord of the limits of honour and decency, etc., etc.' This treaty assured the Company of many rights and privileges as 'a most favoured nation' and considerable business continued to be done with Bagh-dad and the cities of Syria. In 1763 the first British consulate was established here with a Mr. Garden as consul. Never the least thought could then have been in men's minds that in 1916 Basra would become a British-Indian possession and the general headquarters of the most powerful armies that ever left the shores of India for foreign conquest. In 1668 the town was captured by the Turks; it has been the scene of many revolutions; in 1777 it was taken by the Persians after a protracted siege of nine months; in 1787 it was retaken by the Turks and now after years of subjection to the corrupt and desolating Turkish rule, it fell an easy prey to British arms in the early period of this world-war that at present is still raging, when Turkey to her shame and ruin threw in her lot with the Germans against Great Britain and her Allies.

Basra in the old days.

Modern history of Basra.

The taking of Basra by the British-Indian forces.

Early in October 1914, our Government scenting trouble with Turkey, providently sent forward a brigade of British and Indian troops to make a demonstration at the head of the Persian Gulf, prepared to occupy the island of Abadan, as well as the port of Basra. On the 5th November 1914 war was declared against Turkey. On the 22nd November 1914 Basra was occupied without much difficulty by our forces under Lieut.-General Sir Arthur Barrett, who has, it is interesting to note, presented Lord Willingdon as a souvenir of this historic exploit a Turkish military trophy bearing the Sultan's arms and the Imperial *toghru* or cryptogram finely sculptured on a large slab of white stone, which is to be seen in the portico of Government House, Malabar Point. The Governor of Basra who surrendered the town was deported and died lately somewhere in Burma. Basra and its vilayet is British now, an appanage of British India. Exit the Turk and his sterilising misrule!

CHAPTER XLIX.

Description of Basra.

There are no hotels to speak of in Basra to suit anyone used to European ways of living. Up to lately one of the captured Austro-Lloyd's steamers, the Franz Joseph, served as a hotel for officers. Remaining therefore on board the Zayanni as she lay at anchor in Basra harbour, I went ashore in a *bellam* several times and had a good look at both the old city of Basora and its port of Ashaar. Kinnear, who was a great traveller in Eastern lands, in his geography of Persia (a most interesting work) describes Basra 'without contradiction the dirtiest city he had ever seen,' and its condition as I saw it, no way belies the description.

Basra as it stands to-day may be said to be composed of three or rather four distinct portions exclusive of its suburbs.

Description of Basra.

The town proper, the native and British portions of Ashaar which is the port of Basra and the present military occupation or cantonments all along the river bank, some eight miles in extent, from Beyt-Nameh to Margil. The town proper or Basra city is situated over three miles inland, west of the river, towards the end of the great Ashaar creek, which is navigable for *bellams* and other small boats. All traffic to and from the town is carried on by the creek, or by a broad but ill-built carriage road running on the south side of it, called the '*Tarik-es-Sahil*' which means the shore-road or the strand as it is now styled! We visited the old town in a hired victoria. Hack victorias are in great request and we had some trouble in getting one; a very ramshackle concern but it did its duty. Crowds stand at the bridgehead on the Strand Road

The Strand Road.

Hack victorias.

impatiently waiting for an empty victoria and as soon one is espied returning from the old town, there is a run and a rush for it or ever the occupants are out of it, it is stormed and carried by whosoever manages to scramble into it among the first. There is much screaming and objurgation. The old town entered through one of its tumbled-down gates is extensively built, with several decent, large houses, ill-built and partly decaying, with mostly narrow streets and lanes, a couple of large squares, which could be turned into something handsome and pleasant, but at present are not, an open market-place where cattle, donkeys and poultry are exposed for sale on the *Khamsa* or the fifth day of the week, which is the market day throughout the Arab world and where no doubt before and since 'the golden prime of Haroun Al Rashid' was carried on a lively traffic in human flesh. Next we came by a large caravanserai of the usual pattern so often described by travellers in the East, but now used as a civil jail, a sign of British occupation. Not far from this place is a part of the old fortifications, where now 'the gentlemen in khaki' or fierce Panjabis, 'the sword-arm of India,' mount guard. Close by stands a large regular theatre much dilapidated as is the custom with all buildings hereabouts. Here mountebanks, jugglers, dancers of all sorts and characters, strolling players and musicians give performances, which from all accounts are much patronised by the aristocracy and gentry of Basra. Bandman & Co. or any other such wandering followers of Thespis might do good business here whilst the novelty lasted. Pretty actresses, singing and music and above all the art of the 'light fantastic toe' with ample display of 'the human form divine' such as is now so much the fashion even on the very decorous and prudish English stage, would I think take the Arab fancy and entrance his soul immensely and the caterer bids fair to make an early fortune. I believe a cinema or two have already established themselves in Basra city and Ashaar to teach the young Arab idea how to shoot in various novel directions. Sinbad's old

The Old Basra.

The theatre.

town is already humming through a remarkable transformation scene. Passing on we came up on the great bazaars of Basra. These are of considerable size, but vary very little from all such as you see in these Arab and Persian towns of any pretention to importance. I however, always found them interesting and liked rambling about in and out of their ever-intricate thoroughfares and among the various shops and booths, and stalls that give so much life, colour and character to the place and people. Amidst all the variety of trades and professions that so crowd these dim and cool bazaars and serve the convenience of the inhabitants, what I never tired of watching with amused eye are the fragrant cook-shops and little stands kept by itinerant vendors of cooked delicacies. Here like flies round a *halvai's* tray of sweets, clustered a crowd of hungry men and boys who evidently had no pot-boiling at home and took their meals abroad. The fare consisted of roasted meat, hard-boiled eggs, pickles, *mast* or curdled milk and cheeze *a la carte* or dished up incontinently in a heap on half a sphere of the native bread serving as plate and swallowed standing, amidst social chatter, nodding of heads, and gesticulations.

<small>The Basra bazaars.</small>

CHAPTER L.

Asha'ar.

Ashaar or rather the broad creek of Ashaar is the port of Basra and just now the busiest portion of the city of Sinbad. The word or name seems if I mistake not derived from 'Mashaar,' the Arabic for a customs or toll house. At the mouth of the creek on the right-hand side as you pass into it from the river stand the busy Customs house, offices and warehouses, and both banks of it as far as the first bridge, furnished with steps at short intervals half sunk in the muddy ooze and in chronic disrepair. This is the main place for landing and embarking for all coming in by water or having business up and down the river. The creek is tidal and runs between high banks. There are two infirm-looking, grotesque but serviceable wooden bridges spanning it for carriage and foot traffic; these bridges open in the middle for the bagalows and other high-masted boats as they pass up and down. A short way beyond the first bridge, you come to the open country on either side, covered by carefully planted date-tree groves standing within low embankments into which *kannats* or channels are cut to let in the water at high tide from the creek. On the right-hand there is a large building which was used when I saw it, as the newly-started Court of Small Causes, presided over by a military officer and worked no doubt on non-regulation lines so dear to the British bureaucratic head and heart. A Court of wards and a district Court with insolvency jurisdiction are soon to be in full swing here with the inevitable queue of lawyers and touts. The simple Arab as soon as he becomes sophisticated as he is bound to be under the new dispensation, will of all things undoubtedly appreciate the benefits of the insolvency section which allows of

The Creek.

British Courts.

evading his creditors by legal process, without need of incurring a blood-feud, or voluntary exile. Not far from the Court is a seedy-looking, squalid building, difficult to approach at low tide, which was pointed out to me as the best of the many *hamams* or public baths which Basra boasts of and is used by the more respectable residents here whenever inclined to undergo a good scrub. Ordinary dwelling-houses in these Gulf towns manage to do without bathing and other toilet conveniences. The general Arab population evidently are not partial to frequent ablution.

The Hamam.

Leaving this bath-house you come up with the American mission quarters, with their schools, hospital, dispensary, workshops and resident bungalows. In this part of the world and in many parts of Persia the American Presbyterian missions have long been established. The practical good sense, tact and ready tolerance with which their work is conducted makes them welcome and popular and all who have come in contact with them and experienced their benevolent activities speak of them with high appreciation.

The American Mission.

Latterly the Y. M. C. A. have also put up an establishment in Basra to meet, it is said, the spiritual wants of Westerners now fast peopling the banks of the Shat' and to teach the semitic Moslem a more authentic way to Heaven by turning him away from Allah and Mahomed his prophet. At all times of the day the head of the Ashaar creek presents a most animated scene of multicoloured life and movement.

The Y.M.C.A.

The Venice of the East.

It may be compared (*longo intervallo* of course) to the grand canal at Venice and this has procured for Basra its title of the Venice of the East. The crowds of boats, the lumbering lighters and cargo-creepers, the pretty *bellams* especially, being so like the gondola or Venetian *barcola* in shape and movement, the people curiously clad going up or down the water-stairs, the cries of the boatmen, the clear blue sky overhead, the crisp, cold air, all this tends to lend a certain vraisemblance to this description of Basra.

A short acquaintance with actual facts however dispels the brief illusion, and old Sinbad's city is little likely to rival 'the nurseling of the seas' that queens the Adriatic. All the same the busy life and the changing scenes on the broad Ashaar creek are both interesting and entertaining and are so peculiar to the place as to arrest the stranger's attention.

Speaking of the *bellam*, it is the passenger boat of Basra and the Shat-el-Arab from Mohomerah to Kurnah and deserves a short description. Sir Percy Sykes somewhere in his voluminous books of travels quite incorrectly calls it 'a raft,' as if it were like the bloated skin-floats seen on the Indus, or the *kufa* or *gufa*, the circular bitumen-coated leathercovered craft of the upper Tigris, used for ferrying passengers or river-fishing. The *bellam* certainly is not a raft nor anything like a raft. On the contrary it is the prettiest little watercraft to be seen anywhere for moving about in harbour or going on the river. The *bellam* has it seems to me its echo in '*vellam*' which is the name of the small boat used in the back-waters of South Travancore in India. Flat-bottomed, twenty feet or somewhat more in length with two and a half to three in the beam, the *bellam* tapers at both ends which are carved and curved up inwards like ram's horns and coloured or gilded. Prettily painted gray body with dark-red bottom, blue and light green, white and bottle-green in harmonious tints, it has comfortable cushioned seats amidship for two or three persons with canopy or sunshade overhead. Going upstream close in shore it is impelled or punted by two boatmen standing fore and aft with long poles, or it is rowed or sailed downstream or allowed to drift with the tide. Prettier than the sombre gondola, yet equally if not more handy, more like the Istamboli caique,—there are over two thousand of these boats that ply for hire at Ashaar, along the river way and up and down the creeks. Every man of means at Basra and Mohomerah sports his own *bellam* or two for pleasure. It is delightful to be in a *bellam* on the river, morning or evening, in the lovely winter climate of Basra. Its motion is easy, swift and agreeable. *Bellams* of a somewhat larger

The bellam.

build capable of carrying from ten to twenty people are commonly used for passenger service between the principal ports on the Shat?.

CHAPTER LI.

The Town of Ashaar.

The town of Ashaar at the head of the Creek is divided by this waterway into the native Arab or Turkish town on the right and the European business quarters on the left bounded by the Strand Road. In the latter are to be seen many large houses lining the road occupied by various officers and business establishments among which stand the British post and telegraph offices, the military and shipping offices, a branch of the Eastern Bank of India doing excellent business, the police station and the office of the 'Times of Basra,' with its Arab title 'Qal-el-Basra.' By the way this is a very enterprising press bantling consisting of a single sheet of four quarto pages, containing brief war-news, a leading article whenever available and for the rest trade advertisements which I suspect make for necessary subsistence. Its policy seems to be more or less opportunist, nevertheless I wish it success. Perhaps a strong independent paper just now in Mesopotamia however much wanted, *would not pay*. In this part too, further in along a cross-street are several large European shops, with the names of which most people in Bombay are familiar, —Evans Fraser, Leach & Weborney, D. Macropolo, Army & Navy Stores, Richardson & Crudas and others, who having taken time by the forelock are bound to do a roaring business in the present state of affairs in 'Mesopot' (as Tommy irreverently contracts 'that blessed word' into), all over where the class of goods they deal in are in urgent and constant demand and war-prices rule the rate unquestioned and uncontrolled, making their pile while the war blazes. The fronts or outsides of these establishments are by no means in keeping with the palatial ones in

<small>The 'Basra Times'.</small>

<small>European shops.</small>

Bombay in spite of large lettering and some bunting. Along the river bank in this direction of Ashaar are the Government transport, commissariat and other depôts swarming with busy khakhi-clad people in war array.

Ashaar with its busy port is really a town by itself of considerable size with a population that is 'visibly increeasing.' Gradually grown up around the Customs house and the landing-places, it extends a good way northwards with date plantations to the west and the broad river to the east of it. Its fixed as well as moving population is largely Arab. On the right bank of the Creek high up and overhanging it are to be observed a couple of large *kavakhanas* open to all the breezes and furnished with rough wooden straight-back benches of a peculiar square-cut shape and some few stools or tables. These are constantly crowded all day from early morning, and more so I believe till late at night when they are transformed for the nonce into *cafés-chantants*. Anybody interested in life in Basra is likely to see many phases of it in these Arab restaurants where the native habitués congregate in numbers for refreshment, gossip, talking shop, taking their ease or their fill of amusement. They serve the purpose of a rough-and-ready club without one's having to pay any accommodation or entrance fees.

<small>The Kavakhana.</small>

A long, straight, fairly roomy thoroughfare leading away from the first bridge over the creek divides this portion of the town into nearly two equal parts. It is the high street of Ashaar and very interesting for a visitor to potter about in. On either side without any footway, it has a continuation or rows of rather mean looking houses, the ground-floors of which are occupied by native shops and open stalls, intermingled with what are known in India as 'Europe shops,' a new importation. The place appeared already in possession of many petty traders from Bombay. Borahs, Khojahs, some Banias and a few Parsees who calling themselves 'general merchants,' have opened shops for a varied assortment of Indian, Japanese and European goods, such as silks, cloths, hardware, crockery, haberdashery, boots and shoes, oilman's

<small>The high street of Ashaar.</small>

stores, wines and spirits, clocks and watches, all selling at fancy prices. Small tea-shops and eating houses abound in this street till one fancies there must be interminable guzzling and swilling of drinks to keep them all going. The *sakka* or itinerant water seller's occupation is going if not gone. Among these I noticed one something more pretentious than the others, styled 'The Tip-top English Restaurant,' which offered tea, coffee, cold-drinks, ices, pastry and sweets. It did not look inviting. There are here also several tobacconists' shops, whilst a dentist or two, a couple of hakims with indifferent dispensaries and a solitary photographer have started business and appear to be thriving. There is room yet for more of these professionals. Some of our Parsee L. M. & S., M. B. B. S. and 'Dental Surgeons' instead of 'killing flies,' (as the Guzerati expression hath it,) in Bombay could have an excellent opening if they transferred themselves to and settled in Ashaar, with well-stocked dispensaries under smart compounders, providing patent remedies, toilet requisites, etc. The well-to-do Arabs, so long content with carpets and cushions and bare walls are now beginning to follow the foreigner in the matter of household kit and furniture, and tables and chairs, sofas, bedsteads and cupboards of all sorts, pictures, etc., are coming into general request, so that a few of our cabinet-makers and furniture dealers might do worse than take a run to Basra and have a 'chuckla' quarter there all to themselves. The enterprise is worth embarking on. The entire land is devoid of timber suited for building purpose; it is now largely imported from Bombay and Burma and even from Japan; so that business on a large scale with quick returns could be done at Basra in this important article of commerce. The only drawback however for those not born in the country or inured to it, is the atrocious climate of Basra for at least five long months of the year, between early April and end of October, when the torrid heat is extraordinarily severe. As a naval officer expressed it once to Sir Percy Sykes, 'Basra in summer no place for a man with a short neck,'

Good opening for doctors, etc.

The climate of Basra.

and I should say, nor for any with even a long one, except he be born and bred along the Shaṭ. But doubtless these summer conditions so deterrent now will in time be largely mitigated under a saner management of things, by better water-supply, by better housing, by instalation of electric fans, ice factories and tree-planting so as to make Basra a tolerable enough place of residence for Indians at all events. The place offers good openings in many directions. The man who has started a couple of motor-omnibuses between Ashaar and Old Basra is already making his pile whilst another who is running half a dozen cabs and hack victorias is doing a flourishing business. There is room enough for more. This native quarter of Ashaar with its crowded bazaars, its large *kavak-hanas*, its busy Customs' offices, and the bustling thoroughfare above described presents scenes of kaleidoscopic colour and variety, whilst for its miscellaneous and multifarious population it may well be described as a complete Asiatic ethnological museum ever on the move. Every sort and class of Semitic peoples, from the Hadramaut to Baghdad and beyond, from Jeddah and Mecca to Teheran, from the Levant and Egypt, from India, Khelat and Kabul, are represented here. To the student of anthropology Ashaar-cum-Basra with its living specimens, offers and affords a vast and most complete field of study and research. Here in an afternoon's walk you see and jostle against Arabs of the towns, Bedouins of the desert, Turks, Jews, Armenians, Negroes, Persians of the plains and Persians of the wild mountains, Baloochis, Kaboolis, Syrians, Indians, Kurds, Egyptians, gipsies and amongst these may be distinguished by their head-gear and costume Mullas, Softas, Wahabi priests, darvishes, Armenian monks, Israelites and Christian missionaries. To this heterogeneous mass of living flesh is now added by way of extra variety, the frequent presence of the British-Indian militarists in khaki, sepoy and soldier, who have arrived to lord it in their

Marginalia: Cabs and victorias. | An ethnological museum. | The Militarist in khaki.

own land over all these 'Jews, Turks, infidels and heathens' as they esteem the natives of the land to be and mean to treat and turn them to account accordingly. The Arab in Basra generally looks with a troubled mind as he watches,

<small>Our new fellow-subject the Arab.</small>

> 'These lords of human kind pass by,
> Pride in their port, defiance in their eye.'

But the Arab forming the bulk of the natives here and all about the Shatt' is a sensible, long-sighted person, by no means impractical; if inclined at first to exclaim '*la haula wa kavata ila billah*' in deprecation of the changing of things, will yet settle down to the new alien regime and thank Allah for it as he sees and learns the value of the heavy hand along with the contriving and fertile brain which promises to make 'the desert blossom like the rose,' specially if his beliefs are not meddled with and the inlets of his shekels are not too inquisitively obtruded. He never loved or liked the Turk and now that the Oosmanli has been swept away and the Capital of the *dar-el-Khalifah* is in the hands of the British there is no reason why he should not turn out to be a decent and likeable citizen of the Empire that covers half the habitable globe, if only British rule were impressed on the land with tact and good sense and with less and less of that overweening self-importance, haughty aloofness and mischief-brewing superciliousness with which the Britisher for all his many virtues makes himself obnoxious in many lands which a discriminating (let us trust) Providence subjects to his hand.

CHAPTER LII.

The River front at Basra.

The fourth division which makes up the totality of latter-day Basra consists of the exclusive military occupation quarters all along the eight or nine miles of the river frontage chiefly on the right bank of the Shatt', where feverish war activities prevailed when I was there and no doubt still prevail and where a new town has arisen in a few months as if by the waving of an enchanter's wand or rather by the opening wide of Fortunatus' purse, the bottom of which the war administration of the day cares not to fathom. The great war is in evidence along the whole extent of this quarter on water as on land. There you see standing the officers' hospital, the European soldiers' hospital, the Native troops' hospital, their staff's resident quarters, the offices of the naval and military departments, the harbour master's and the berthing master's houses and establishment, lines and lines of barracks built and being built, military post and telegraph offices, electric instalation, commissariat sheds, stores and cold storage, artillery depôts, officers' club and messes, soldiers' canteens, nurses' and medical officers' residences, railway premises with sheds, stores, sidings, offices and stations and the B. I. S. N. Co.'s offices. Busy wharves and docks and landing jetties are there and more are building where never before was known a wharf or fit landing-place. The din of war is resounding in every direction and work, work, work is going on at high pressure. The scenes as I saw them were full of animation and busier than any hive could be. It was just at the time that the powerful attacks were being delivered again against the Turks in their turn beleaguered in ever-to-be famous Kut-el-Amara and the air was full of rumours and stories of British

A new Town.

successes, though nothing definite was known then even at Basra, so near as it is to the scenes of active operations. The riverside was crowded with shipping of every size and description. Basra in all the centuries of its existence for the first time now sees and realises things and doings it never could even have dreamt of before. There were to be seen troops landing, troops embarking, troops marching, great floating steam-cranes transferring great guns and whole railway trucks and steam-launches from ship to shore, locomotive engines puffing their way with full trains behind them between Mergil and Kornah, motor-cars, motor-lorries, motor-cycles and bicycles busy plying or scurrying this way and that; the ungainly p. bs. or paddle-boats and stern-wheelers churning up the river waters; huge hospitalships at anchor, ablaze as the sun goes down with red, green and white lights; monster steam-dredgers, enormous wide-gaping iron barges each fit to carry fifty tons of cargo. Besides these are to be seen now and again the marvel of the day, aeroplanes vaster than the fabled roc, manœuvring up in the air with pattering wings, fulfilling the poet's prescience of 'airy navies grappling in the central blue.' All this sudden transformation, extraordinary and amazing, wrought by this long catalogue of marvels leaves the Basraite agape with wonder, like a second Rip Van Winkle or the sleepers of Ephesus shaken out of their slumber of ages. And methinks he had better wake up and bestir himself all he is worth, else there is every chance of his being pushed to the wall by his more wide-awake and enterprising Indian fellow-subjects.

War activities.

At the northern end of this new quarter or new town of Basra, is the village of Mergil, a sort of pleasure resort of the people of Basra. It is now turned into a special close reserve or preserve for Europeans only such as this war has brought into Basra. Here and around here the hollowed out date-groves have been extensively cleared of their trees, and silt and mud dredged from the river-bed is pumped by powerful steam-dredgers over the embankments to level up and form new land for building purposes. Here at this end is the terminus of the railway incessantly pushed on

Mergil.

to Kornah, Baghdad, Samara and further northward. Electric light illuminates all this quarter. The immense solitudes of the desert that was, where lived and moved or rather crawled and hibernated a scanty population of uncivilised nomads is now all overanimated with new vitality such as was never known, nor pictured before and the conservative Basraite who leaves everything to Kismet needs stand rubbing his eyes, blinking, gaping and lost 'in cogitibundity of cogitation.' The untold expenditure, which nobody ventures to calculate or dares to question, already so lavishly incurred and still being daily incurred in so solidly and substantially building up this British Basra quarter, whilst it astonishes the natives, raises in them at the same time reasonable hopes that all this really means the permanence of the British occupation from which they are evidently not averse. They rather are looking forward to this consummation and doubtless are quite prepared to renounce the Turk and all his works and to throw in their lot with their new masters. This being so, it would be as many aver a serious blunder from every view-point ever to hand over again all this territory conquered at such enormous sacrifice of blood and treasure to the ever unregenerate and treacherous Turks. In this view of it I cannot do better than close this chapter by quoting what Sir Arthur, Lawley so well puts it in his recent little work 'Mesopotamia.' 'It is certain,' he says, 'that if in an ill-starred moment when the war draws to an end we vacate the land, our withdrawal will be regarded as a betrayal of men whom we have wheedled into allegiance and will have the worst possible effect on our Mahomedan subjects throughout the Empire.' To this may be added the concluding words of the address of Lord Hardinge when he visited Basra in January 1915:—'I have come here to see local conditions for myself: You are aware that we are not engaged single-handed in this great struggle and we cannot lay down plans for the future without an exchange of views with other great Powers, but I can

The Arabs' expectation.

Sir Arthur Lawley on the situation.

Lord Hardinge's promise.

hold out the assurance that the future will bring you a more benign rule.' The Basra people would not be mistaken if they accept these clear words as a promise not to hand them over to the tender mercies of the irreclaimable Turk, and on the full fulfilment of which they are entitled to count.

CHAPTER LIII.

British Military Rule in Basra.

Khartoum, far down the Nile, was once, as we know, a malaria-infested spot amidst wildernesses of sand, a prey to rival hordes of wild, contending, ignorant, factious fanatics, cut off from all vivifying civilised life. In some nineteen years, since Omdarman sealed the fate of the Mahdhists, it has under British rule blossomed into a beautiful, progressive and prosperous city, well deserving the name now given to it—'The Garden City of Egypt.' There is no reason then why Basra similarly situated on the Shat', sunk to insignificance and ill-fame by long years of inertness and misrule, should not look up and be regenerated into a rival of Khartoum, if things proceed and eventuate as one expects them to do under the new and happier conditions it now finds itself in.

Martial law.

Since the Turk has been thrust out, the place with its environs is under the sway of a British military Governor and a Deputy Governor and for the present is governed by martial law. This is a necessity no doubt under war conditions, but it would be well if it be tempered by goodwill, tact, and practical good sense. Already the *vis inertiæ* that so long brooded over the land is giving way before new activities as is seen by numerous signs of improvement and progress in many directions. Some of these signs may be trivial but it is the lifted straw that shows which way the wind blows.

A change in the face of things.

Anything like a reliable town police was unknown in Basra before the advent of the English. Even before sundown it was the enforced custom for all house-doors to be closed and securely locked. After 4 p.m. no women of any respectability could safely venture into the streets.

Roughs and foot-pads abounded and had it all their own way. The police was inefficient, the courts corrupt. There was no such thing as street lighting. Sanitation was unknown, no attempt was made to make or mend roads. All this is now changed. In Ashaar and Basra European soldiers and Indian sepoys now regularly patrol and police the streets and the river by day and night. Every body feels and must be thankful for the security this has brought about for person and property. At night kerosine lamps well-lighted are put up on posts, or hang down from hooks or brackets projecting from house-walls at proper intervals and at convenient corners. The English quarter is lighted by electricity. Scavengers sweep the roads at stated times and cart away all dirt and rubbish. New roads are laid out and old ones taken in hand and turned to something like carriage-ways. Cinders and boiler sweepings from the steamships afford cheap and excellent road material, so the same is commandeered and utilised accordingly. A couple of steam-rollers (when they arrive) will surely provide Basra with as good roads as could be desired. Motor-cycles, the emblem of speed and despatch, are already to be seen in the streets of Ashaar and the Strand Road. The native Arab is already taking to the bicycle. It was amusing to see a large Arab, his flowing overgown well tucked in round his waist and with sandalled-shoon, treadling a safety-cycle. Street-boards showing names of streets and localities in Roman and Arabic characters are put up at obvious ends and corners and some of these names, more than most things, argue British possession in a telling way, as for instance, 'Governor's Road,' 'Emperor's Road,' 'Oxford Street,' 'Jaipur Street,' 'Crooked Lane,' 'Club Road,' 'Church Street,' 'Hyde Park Corner.' Other signs are not wanting to emphasise the new order of things. The Gymkhana and the Club are already there. The Y. M. C. A. is there as I have said before. A substantial edifice in the shape of a church dedicated to the patron saint of England, or some other equally efficacious saint is not yet

Arab on bicycle.

Signs of British occupation.

erected, but it is surely bound to be there ere long, if not there since my recent visit. A race-course is already there at Makina in the direction of Mergil run according to the W. I. T. C. rules, with a couple of totalizators and all the needful turf accompaniments to make horse-breeding profitable and edifying too, as providing object-lessons in popular morals. The clergyman and the jockey are estimable English institutions and ever go hand-in-hand to indicate a British possession. Race days are instituted which the people consider and sanctify as public holidays, when all Basra, Ashaar, Mohomerah, Abadan and other neighbouring places flock incontinently to Makina where the hippodrome is, to take part in Basra's sport of kings. Wherever British rule extends, prestige, that bugbear or bogie whichever you care to call it by, is of course set up as a worshipful fetish and so it is now in Basra. Orders are out and strictly enforced, according to which the *pas* must be conceded to the European, soldier or civilian cockscomb or brass-hat, chief or sub, by the aborigines of the place high or low. The *topee* or helmet is the too obtrusive symbol of foreign sway, almost to the extent (*absit omen*) of Gesler's hat in the market place of Althdorp. If two or three Britishers choose, as they usually do, to walk abreast in the narrow streets, the Arab or other nondescript native or stranger must nil he will he take the wall. If some of these swells coming riding in a hack-victoria, and another victoria with 'native' gentlemen comes from the opposite way, the latter must pull up to let the all-imposing, over-exacting sahibs pass. Soldiers stand sentinels at the ends of the bridge, which connects north and south Ashaar, to prevent the natives using the main or central broad passage when a sahib, the all-highest entity, is on it or about to cross; they the erstwhile owners of the country must wait or crowd on to the very narrow strip of planked footway on either side of the bridge till the sahib and even the *statutory* Anglo-Indian leisurely stalks over. The hack-driver and the *bellamchi* are required under penalties to give preference to this sort of European fare even if his conveyance is already engaged by a

<small>Race Course.</small>

<small>British prestige.</small>

native. A Mr. Swayne in a volume recently placed before the public and much puffed by some too friendly critic, recommends violence as necessary and right to keep the *bellamchi* and his like in order if inclined (according to the European's fancy) to be disrespectful, or to claim more as his due than what the latter chooses to allow. He cites with approval a clergyman thrashing a native and a Russian officer throwing another into the Shat' for some fancied slight or want of the servility the lordly Westerner thinks fit to exact. The priest surely forgot the teachings of his Master and the Russian was what he is bound to be—a *kuzzak*. Yet our English author recommends these samples of Christian meekness of spirit as meet for imitation. This same sapient Englisher, wise in his own conceit, gives it as his opinion that in a country like Mesopotamia indulgence in alcohol is 'humanising in effect,' and proceeds to clinch this counsel of perfection by saying that if the prophet forbade it, 'it is worth remembering he permitted other things.' If report be trusted both alcohol as well as the 'other things' are much indulged in in our new possessions on the Shat' in a way that is of course not quite on the surface. This unthinking truculence which the author above referred to so inaptly and so fatuously recommends is, I find, aptly illustrated in a cartoon of a recent issue of the 'Basra Times,' where is exhibited a British subaltern or clerk in shirt-sleeves, pretending to speak to his Hindu attendant in the vernacular and misunderstanding the reply, violently kicks the unfortunate servant out of the room. This may be a comic presentment of British prowess and prestige, but is apt to lead to tragic consequences. This elegant cartoon is headed 'Budged,' and if the newcomers do not mind their ps. and qs., this sort of thing might bring about their budging in earnest from the country, *where the Arab is not* likely to be so long-suffering as the Indian has so far been. Anyhow, all I and others who care to give a right thought to it can say is that the sooner such and other similar bureaucratic methods and antics for enforcing respect

Reflections. and upholding of prestige are discouraged and discountenanced, the better will it be for the peace and prosperity of these new provinces which the fortunes of war have added, let us hope permanently, to the British Empire. British rule promises, in fact assures peace, security and prosperity to this Arab land. The native of it on his part is willing evidently to accept the new regime and it is up to the Britisher to see whether it is worth while to make it acceptable to him when the question of self-determination arises after the war. The pre-war and present notion of stubborn swollen-headed superiority of race, so pregnant with peril and mischief, had best therefore be sternly put out of fashion.

CHAPTER LIV.

A Day off at Asha'ar.

Since Basra has passed into British hands and the Parsees like trade follow the flag, several of them have come up and are resident there, mostly in Asha'ar. Many are engaged in business which the war with its urgent and endless demands largely provides,—business which if report speaketh true is made profitable by judicious or unscrupulous palm-manuring which is looked upon as a necessity and a quite licit incentive to business. Persians who call it *moodakhal*, are adepts in practising it and it is said the Shah himself, the shadow of God, 'exacts it without fail whenever he extends mercy to a culprit or bestows a title on a courtier.' Others are employed in Government and other offices. A friend among them who lived in Asha'ar, chumming with other co-religionists, invited us to have a day ashore and we very gladly availed ourselves of the kind invitation which promised a pleasant outing. The weather was ideal for a holiday, we punted up in a pretty *bellam* and landed near the Beit-Vakil which is used as some sort of war-work office. The transport and commissariat and shipping departments have their habitats here. The sepoy and soldier, officer, non-com. and private, inspector, sub-inspector, lascar, porter, carter, muleteer moved to and fro, all in the dusty war-paint of drab or buff khaki, top-boots, putties, belts, straps, side-arms and resplendent in a profusion of distinctive brass buttons and regulation head-gear. Bullock-drawn commissariat carts, officers' horses, mules, narrow-gauge railway trucks all signifying vividly war and battles added to the bustle that prevailed.

The Moodakhal.

Beit-Vakil.

Crossing the great Creek, we disembarked at the customs' stairs, where quite different scenes met us, bespeaking trade and commerce, with moving phases of life in Basra.

<small>The Customs' stairs.</small>

Here the right-hand shore for a considerable way is invaded by a multitude of dhows, lighters and bagalows four and five deep laden with merchandise which flows in incessantly. The prows of some of the dhows standing high above water are gaily decorated in loud colours. Consignees and boatmen were busy unloading, tallying, transporting, stacking the arriving cargoes, amidst much jabbering but without any undue haste or expenditure of energy. The early forenoon here is the busiest time. Passing along the quays we walked up the long uneven road or lane by the sides of which is held the Asha'ar bazaar of market produce and other commodities; not much of a bazaar to speak of, but interesting nevertheless. The road joins the high-street as I have named it and before described and to the other side of which is the Arab merchants' quarter with its narrow, crooked lanes. Here we visited the house and office of Mr. Abd-ul-Jabbar 'the servant of the all-powerful.'

<small>Mr Abd-ul-Jabbar.</small>

This gentleman is a very well-to-do Arab merchant doing extensive business in Basra, with Bombay, Baghdad and other places. He is the Agent of the P. G. N. Co. He was of course a Turkish subject and liable to conscription. He was in Baghdad when Turkey entered the war, but managed to escape in time to Basra. If the Turks have the upperhand again he risks being shot. Meantime considering his antecedents the all-seeing eye of the military C. I. D. is on him it is likely enough. The poor man is like the flying-fish, between the shark and the sea-eagle. He is possessed of much house and landed property and has considerable influence. He certainly should be met with considerate treatment. He received us in a very pleasant and friendly manner. Middle aged, rather thick-set, good-looking and genial, he has the reputation of being a capable and smart man of business. A slight rain had rendered the entrance, inner court and stair-way up to his office wet, muddy and slippery, giving the place the appearance of not having been swept or cleansed for a week or longer. Doors, windows, walls and floors stood much in need of a good spring cleaning. We had to pick our way up gingerly. The office is furnished with modern furniture but kept and used as it seemed in Arab fashion, with round-topped desk, swivel chair and a couple of cushioned seats much used and polish worn off, there were besides some high stiff-back benches against a side-wall of the peculiar Arab make, all right angles with hard seats such as a Persian would describe as *shelwar-dur* or 'breeches bruiser.' A clock too there was that didn't go and a date-rack that stood at 30th November though it was Xmas week. Cigarette ends, ashes, waste-paper littered the floor. All showed slovenly but comfortable disarray, dirt and dinginess, characteristic of the innate or inert simplicity of Arab conservative life and liking, which eschews over-spruceness and all hygienic exaction and which the Stoic perhaps would justify and admire, Mr. Jabbar's views on war results in Basra so far as they prevail would be interesting if he were open to interviewing. Arabs and Aghas came in sipped coffee, had a pull at the *kalyoon* or *chilam* or sucked cigars, did business and went out. All

A modern Cæsar.

the while Mr. Jabbar talked polite nothings with us, and went on with his work signing papers, ordering his clerks like another Cæsar in a small way and smoking an interminable length of successive cigarettes, a good heap of which lay loosely on his desk, ready at hand. Coffee being served we made a 'tactical retreat.' Here we met our host of the day, with whom we perambulated the streets which run to Mergil and Zobeir, looking this way and that and nosing things in general; visited old Basra of which we made a general inspection. The diversity of the Basra vulgus in face, figure and costume made street life interesting, though the absence of the gentler sex made it something

Women in the streets.

monotonous. A few women and these of the lower orders probably, were to be seen about muffled up from head to foot in their dingy dark or indigo-dyed *chader* and *rouband*, which ugly and ungraceful though they be are signs of strict respectability, so that even those of them who are

Christian converts or Armenians go similarly swathed, distinguishable only by being smartly shod in Parisian or Viennese footwear and hosiery and by their more sprightly movement. A few *demimondaines* however, whom one came across here and there in twos and threes, lent colour and piquancy to the scene. These bedizened, rouge-bedaubed gentry, flaunting in gay attire of many colours, their necks, ears and noses, wrists, fingers and ankles ostentatiously loaded with much cheap and tawdry jewellery and faces embelished with *kohl* and beauty spots pretty freely discovered were easily signalised. Much the same are these doubtless as those whom Solomon admonishes against, 'subtil of heart; loud and stubborn and whose feet abide not in their house; who now are without, now in the street and at every corner.' It shows how human nature is evidently much the same at all times and in every clime and condition however old grows this terrestrial world. As we loitered by the road I remarked the very large number of pedestrians, Arabs, Jews, private soldiers and sepoys, commissariat employés and others, who sported wristwatches; the mystery was explained when I found that in these latter days a petty trader from Bombay foreseeing good profits, made his way to Basra with quite a cargo of metal wrist-watches at Rs. 2-8 a-piece, which catching the local fancy he disposed of at Rs. 9 a-piece and a bit over. The bold venture deserved all the profiteering, with the result that every third way-farer you meet in Ashaar is possessed of a watch and is learning the value of time. Among the new small shopkeepers in Basra I was told there are some twenty-five petty watchmakers, who at present are doing good business. Here too as in Manamah I saw boys of all ages regardless of traffic making rushes in the streets and round the corners playing the one outdoor game they seem to take to,—whip-topping. The youngsters who kept their pegs or whelks lashed up longest were the heroes of the moment, the by-standers showing much interest in the game. By one o'clock we reached our friend's house where we were very pleased to see several of the Basra Parsees

<small>Watches on wrists.</small>

<small>Street game.</small>

invited to meet us and a very pleasant, cheerful, contented lot we found them. An entertaining and jovial company it was, with whom we discussed and discoursed on Basra conditions, Basra politics, and the present and future of Parsees now consorting and congregating in the newest of British possessions. Among other items of information we were told that the Basra Parsees have collected a fund for the purchase and upkeep of a burial ground, which is located some way out of Ashaar and was secured with some difficulty through the good offices of the military commandant. They were led to do this good work on the first Parsee dying in Basra, who at the time of his death employed all alone in some works at some distance found to have been buried by his Arab attendants necessarily without any of the prescribed Zarthosti ceremonies, and in a remote and abandoned spot. News of this mischance leaking out the Parsees were much exercised in mind, their religious feelings harrowed. So they hastily set about acquiring the Parsee *Sonapore* (abode of sleep) or 'khoomoolistan' (abode of oblivion), obtained an exhumation permit, set out in a small party, after great trouble discovered the wild and lonely spot, identified the body as assuredly as circumstances permitted, and being overtaken by night, buried it like Sir John Moores', 'darkly at dead of night, with the lantern dimly burning'; doubtless 'few and short were the prayers' said by the burying party who all the while were in mortal tremor, fearing a raid by priestly fanatics. Whether there was on this mournful occasion any 'struggling moon-beam's misty light,' as the reverend gentleman poetically misstates it in his one immortal poem, the deponents said not and I missed inquiring. Anyhow the Basra Parsees religiously and bravely did their duty and if it be clear that the body so transferred to the new consecrated ground be that of a brother Zarthosti, they have intervened in time with rites and mantras to save its soul from being ravished by the fearful *Darooghnesha*, so nervously dreaded by Parsees. The Basra Parsees who have acted so piously deserve very great credit and commendation, and their co-religionists in Bombay will, it is hoped, liberally support the fund aforesaid. After doing full justice to the excellent breakfast, Parsee style, our host most hospitably provided and which a cook from Surat borrowed from a neighbour, quite a genius in his line, had prepared to perfection, we with our host and some of the company finished off the day by a delightful run up to Mergil in a motor-launch which Mr. Jabbar obligingly placed at our disposal, and a very interesting and merry excursion it was. The great Shat' was alive with every imaginable description of boat, ship and steamer showing specimens derived from hoary antiquity to the present day and which made a most complete marine museum. Our motor-launch in charge of an Arab engineer and an Arab stoker, was an ancient second-hand machine that had seen much rough wear and tear, and though threatening momentary explosion, did the trip without serious mishap, with only one breakdown midstream when the rudder got dislocated. The mischief, however, was set to right in a most intrepid manner by the stoker, who held back by his ankles by the engineer, leaned over the low stern bulwarks, plunged head-down in the water and re-adjusted the rudder or whatever it was that had unshipped itself and brought us to a standstill, just as we were thinking of calling for a tug to tow us back again. We got back to the Zaiyanni in time for dinner having thoroughly enjoyed our outing thanks to our good friends in Basra.

A trip up the River.

Intrepid Arab stoker.

CHAPTER LV.

Life on the Shatt'el Arab.

Life on the broad and easy-flowing river of the Arabs just now in the year of grace 1917 is one of constant variety and animation 'from morn to noon, from noon to dewy eve.' Early in the morning ere yet the sun is well above the horizon are to be seen small boats, deftly rowed or poled mostly by peasant women, girls and boys. These females as seems to be the case with rustics, do not cover their faces and such as I saw *did not* require to. They come from up and down the river with milk and other dairy produce, poultry, vegetables, fruit and fuel to Ashaar and Basra, evidently doing good business. A bold, gay and laughing lot, finding ready market at the hands of Tommy, and Jack and lascar. *Bellams* of all sizes busily ply on the waters from creek to creek or to and from Mohomerah and up the river with men intent on business, passengers passing from place to place, officers and orderlies hastening on war errands. The *bellamchi* never realised such custom before. There is no regular steam-boat passenger service on the Shatt' yet, though it is bound to come, if not by now already there, and displace the leisurely *bellam* and the toilsome lugger. Large cumbersome river-craft, cargo-laden are constantly in sight sailing slowly southward, or being laboriously towed upstream. Sometimes and not an infrequent sight now on this ancient river, a steam-launch is seen to give these old boats a friendly tug. The native method of towing along and up the tow-path on the left bank is novel and peculiar to a stranger's eye. A part of the crew, taking it in relay gangs, harnessing themselves with the ends of the tow-ropes, go toiling up the bank, trodden smooth and firm by constant use, but the main tow-line is passed through or spliced to the top of the

<small>Towing of boats.</small>

single tall mast. This method gives the boat an equable position in the stream and prevents it sagging, zigzagging or bumping into the banks. Occasionally you see a solitary angler standing or wading waist-deep in the water, fishing, a picture of undisturbing imperturbability, 'the badge of all his tribe' ever since the world took to catching of fish. There are to be seen low-lying flat boats floating listlessly by, overlaid with heaps of river-reeds and the tall grasses that line the banks and such as are much used for building native huts and sheds and even rafts in case of need, the half-naked marshman or reed-collector seated idly at the stern making a precarious living. The Armageddon still going on has altered the face of things. All along the eight miles and more of the Ashaar water-front there is unceasing stir and movement, where undisturbed once reigned Asiatic calm or sluggishness and the deep silence of death-like sleep. At the time I was there I off and on counted more than thirty large steamers moored in a long line at a time on the river. Not a day without some moving out and others crowding in. Constant was the motion and commotion. Troopships there were and transports, hospitalships, monitors, warships, stern-wheelers, low paddle-steamers, huge iron barges, monster floating cranes and steam dredgers, not counting the various small river crafts. Work, work was the order of the day, active, regular, unabating, bringing with it an awakening such as neither the urban nor the riparian dwellers of the Shatt' have known, seen or felt since at least the days of the magnificent Caliphs. Over three thousand artisans and labourers are reported to be daily employed here on the construction of a mass of public works, which seem to betoken permanent ownership. In and out among the big boats flew the steam-launches and diminutive motor-boats, with a rattle of engines and screaming of whistles, raising wavelets in the once placid river from shore to shore. On holiday afternoons, more so in the cold weather, the river becomes additionally lively, when pleasure parties in many a gay *bellam* resort to the many pretty gardens

The angler and reed-gatherer.

The shipping on the River.

Holiday-makers.

and orchards that are to be found on both banks and specially at the picturesque mouths and sides of some of the broader creeks like the Khandak and the Basra, to which places mountebanks, musicians, dancers, acrobats, provision-dealers *et hoc genus omne* find their way to amuse the holiday-makers. Often too now-a-days the riverside is much enlivened by parties of European nurses, members of the hospital staffs and officers off-duty in coquettish uniform or in regimental finery, coming out in the evenings or by moonlight in *bellams,* motor-boats or launches to take the air and have a bit of gay time to relieve nostalgia and vary the monotony of their perhaps too strenuous lives in this foreign clime. In the hot months again the banks of the Shatt' are alive with camps of the nomads, who to avoid the scorching heat of the desert come and tent up by the cooler waterside, accompanied by their herds of sheep, horses and buffaloes, creating quite a different aspect of the life on the river. Much bargaining, buying and bartering then goes on. By October these wild and uncouth visitors fold up their tents and disappear as quietly as they came, to fresh fields and pastures new or to camping grounds of old. Such are the river scenes that the curious visitor views as he paces the steamer's deck or strolls on either bank. The jolly sea-gulls are always there sporting on the waters or on the wing in varying formations and numbers, adding much to the liveliness and beauty of the scenes. As night deepens perfect peace prevails. No movement of ships is at present allowed after sunset. As Milton puts it, 'Silence is pleased,' broken casually by the throb of the distant Arab drum and the tinkle of some rustic tambourine from a festive village or the brief tolling of bells on boardship, and the sudden chorus of frogs echoing to the scream of a prowling shackal. Later as time speeds on and things have settled down and this ever-to-be-execrated *German* war is ended, its alarms and rumours hushed and heard no more, the Shatt' will undoubtedly witness regattas, swimming matches and other fluvial sports such as make the Westerners bear 'the white man's burdens' with equanimity under Orient skies. Whatever necessity (if it ever should) arise diplomatically to restore Baghdad to the discredited Turks, the Shatt' from Kornah to the sea must remain a British river in the fullest sense of the word, the Basra vilayet a British possession, and the ancient emporium of the Caliphs an inalienable part and parcel of the British Empire. So mote it be!

CHAPTER LVI.

Views and Conclusions.

My journey is coming to a close; but before concluding, some sort of a resumé of impressions and conclusions would not be out of place here. If war, and such a fearful war as the one still being fought out, is at all times full of horrors, losses, sorrows, and sufferings, it has yet its compensations too, if only nations and peoples are inspired and moved from on High to set about it, when Peace is restored, in the right way and the native dwellers of the countries that have been overrun by hostile armies be allowed and guaranteed their right of self-determination by some fair, free, just and effective method or scheme of settlement. My view of it is that under the operation of some such scheme, well conceived and firmly carried out, many a state and people would gladly renounce and give up its pre-war masters and status and make choice of newer, more congenial and therefore more preferable conditions. When this comes about, as it will and must, I make no doubt the country of Mesopotamia and its adjacent territories from which the Turks are driven out will readily declare for British Rule. Much the larger majority of the population of these ancient lands is Arab. Now the Arab is clearly sick of Turkish rule, young or old; more so now than ever before, seeing how all Turkey is bolstered up and run by the blood-and-iron methods of the modern Hun whose vassal it has been reduced to be. The extensive land of the Hedjaz has definitely thrown off the Turkish yoke; all Syria and Palestine are distinctly anti-Turk at heart and are only waiting with eager hope for the victorious peace and triumph of democracy which is bound to come, to renounce their allegiance to

Law of compensation.

Self-determination.

British Rule for Mesopotamia.

Other Arab lands and Turkey.

a power that has so long oppressed and impoverished them with a rod of iron and the hand of spoliation; the Arab states along the Persian Gulf and outside it are to all intents and purposes subject to British control. All Egypt, from the mouths of its great Blue River right away to its distant sources, is practically British and is no longer under a Khedive subordinate to the Sultan, but under a Sultan of her own, independent of the once Sublime Porte, owning the supreme direction of Great Britain. Armenia, rescued by the Russians, is now in open revolt against the re-entry of her former abhorred rulers; the kingdom (as it is called) of Cyprus no longer recognizes even in a shadowy way the Sultan's supremacy; it is absolutely British. Under these circumstances it really becomes unthinkable that the land of the three great rivers that flow *en masse* into the Persian Gulf, wrenched away by force of British-Indian arms from Turkey at such immense sacrifices should ever revert to a power that has misused it for centuries, exploited it for its own selfish ends and uses and has finally lost it by the ordeal of battle challenged by itself and fairly fought out. It will be a most reprehensible thing and a most egregious and sinful blunder if British statesmen or rather the statesmen of the Empire should ever, weakly yielding to diplomatic bluff and bluster, or giving in to any addle-pated regard for Turkish sensibilities, allow the Empire to be shorn of any part of Mesopotamia now securely held by it in perpetual fee, by a right that originates no doubt in conquest, but which will be surely 'broad-based on the people's will,' so that nothing can gainsay it and no power be at liberty to dispute it. The sick-man of Europe, more than ever invalided now, deserves no considerate treatment. Turkey amply deserves the dismemberment she has met with by her own insane subservience to German dictation and her gross want of good-faith. She is body and soul under the trampling heel of her Hun masters. No reform is possible under Turkish rule. The Turk

Egypt, Armenia, Cyprus.

Circumstances require a new regime.

The duty of British statesmen.

The sick-man of Europe.

has over and over again approved himself incapable of accomplishing moral, political or any other re-generation. It may well then be assumed that the British Empire will be enlarged in the near East by the annexation of these new provinces and the great questions that thus will arise are as to the ways and means and methods whereby the new acquisition could and should be organised and administered so as to enrich the Empire, add to its prosperity and increase its power to extend and spread the blessings of freedom, order and civilization in these new directions. All this of course depends on the skill, the energy and above all the wisdom of the Empire's rulers and governors and their will strenuously exercised to think out and do the right thing by and in the truest interests of the peoples of these new possessions now committed to their charge. This means the introduction of a government on broad and liberal lines according to the best of British traditions, a government that confers all legitimate freedom, secures and promotes the people's confidence by trusting them; maintains inviolate their well-established rights, customs, beliefs and privileges, such of course as do not offend against morals, and are not detrimental to the State; and makes it one of its chiefest considerations to spread liberal education throughout the country, to encourage and support industrial enterprises, and extend and promote trade and commerce in all directions. The Arab, as I have said, is a long-headed, sensible fellow, and so long as he is not rubbed the wrong way and given thoughtless cause for irritation, he promises to turn out a tractable, loyal and useful citizen of the Empire, quite unlikely to look back and pine for Turkish rule, now so discredited all over the Arab world. Honest, independent-minded, if somewhat conservative, the Arab is very different to the fanatic and cruel Turk, to the miserly Armenian, to the supple and knock-knee'd Persian and the Jew who worships his money-bags. Carefully and tactfully handled and governed, Mesopotamia under her changed con-

The great questions.

The new Government.

The Arab is amenable.

If properly handled.

ditions is bound to respond to the management of her new masters in a manner that must enure to their mutual benefit and to the greater glory of the Empire. These are the thoughts that crowd the mind of any one who studiously considers recent events, which are the results of this stupendous and ruthless *German* war, and watches the movements martial, civil and political at the great base of the present military operations at Basra and its neighbourhood, as well as in India. Much will have to be done, but nothing that *could not* be done before the new acquisitions could be socially, financially and politically beneficial and profitable. Expert opinion has already pronounced in no equivocal voice their great possibilities. Where the silence and death-grip of the desert brooded and prevailed under Turk, Mongal, Tartar and other marauders, the land of the great rivers was in early times famous for the remarkable fertility of its soil.

<small>Reflections.</small>

<small>The possibilities of Mesopotamia.</small>

<small>Reviving agriculture.</small>

This can surely be now revived, restored and even augmented a hundredfold in various productive ways by the latest methods of up-to-date agriculture with scientific irrigation and the newest engineering skill and training. Trade and commerce which once greatly flourished in these regions so as to satisfy the vast and instant demands of the far-extending Roman Empire, could certainly be made to flourish again and to a far greater extent too, provided the same is manœuvred and promoted by a far-sighted, frank and generous policy of give and take. In this respect as regards opening of new markets the following views of a recent writer on China, Mr. E. H. Parker, are worth quoting, considering and following. They apply with equal force to the new or British Mesopotamia, as they call 'attention to the neglect on the part of British trade generally to revise its methods; especially in the direction of advertising, preparing intelligible price-lists, visiting likely customers on the spot, granting less rigid terms of credit, shaking off compradoric strangulation, treating the native trader

<small>Trade and commerce.</small>

<small>Views on markets in China applicable.</small>

more courteously and more indulgently, and so on.' He holds up to admiration and imitation the more effective methods on the lines above indicated of the wily, pushful and ingratiating though masterful and unscrupulous Teuton, and if British commerce in the mid-rivers land is to prosper and flourish to the fullest extent possible, the author strongly deprecates the 'old "sit still at the chief port and as to inland depend upon the compradore" system,' and recommends the taking to heart of the lessons set by the German rivals and to a system 'of more hustle and energy.' As he says, there must be the 'taking of more pains and the bestowing of more intelligent thought in the conduct of business than the conservative and unimaginative British trader of the old school' is accustomed to. The business to meet the demand for 'foreign fancies' which is sure to arise, must be so conducted as to attract and 'take hold of the people and thrive. It must be on more ready and adaptable methods and not the up-to-date so to say British trader's . . . stand-offish ways and whims. There must be rousing energy, far-seeing and industrious meeting of local calls and needs.' If then new markets are to be opened in Mesopotamia and all around there such as will be largely remunerative and help fully to compensate and recoup the vast war expenditure that is incurred with closed eyes, the Government, the merchant and the trader, British and Indian, must combine, accept the views and conclusions above quoted and work together on sound lines such as will make the new possessions commercially prosperous by making their markets as highly productive and within as short a time as possible. Besides the essential mutual good-will and good understanding between the old countries and the new additions conducive to this end, the opening up of cheap and ready communications by rail and river, and possibly too by air, postal parcel and money-order, telegraphic and telephone facilities, equable and steady exchange, freedom from needless red-tape checks and restrictions, and a thorough revision of fiscal laws and rules will have to be introduced, seen to and worked on practical

What new conditions require to be done.

and generous lines if this 'consummation so devoutly to be wished' is to be brought about on which must mainly depend the future full development of this latest and most interesting accretion to the British Raj, as regards progress, prosperity and success. In fine, no tinkering modifications of the methods of Turkish rule or misrule could work out the real regeneration of Mesopotamia. A strong, stable, capable, liberal and honest Government such as it could count on and find acceptable under British-Indian regime bids fair to restore it to its pristine greatness and prosperity. Under such a Government it has a bright and hopeful future, with Baghdad, or Bhagoodata, the God-given (as some scholars make out its name) as its Capital eclipsing the fame and glories of the Caliphs and with Kornah, Basra and Fao as its world-renowned emporiums.

Future of Mesopotamia.

The language question too in these new provinces already arouses inquiry and is one that promises considerable philological interest and so not to be lost sight of. The extension of the Empire in what may be called middle-Asia, whether under the Indian administration or the Colonial, must of necessity extend the use of Hindustani, India's *lingua franca*. This most generally used of Indian languages, Urdu or the language that owes its origin to the Mongol hordes or camps, has already to a small extent found its way in the bazaars on the Gulf shores, where many petty Indian traders have gone and settled. If trade follows the flag, language follows trade and this fact will now be largely developed by the immense influx into middle-Asia of Indians whether as soldiers, civilians, camp followers and office-dependents, almost all of whom more or less speak Urdu, making it the necessary means of their communications and intercourse with their new fellow-subjects. It will afford the linguistic student a fine and interesting subject of study and inquiry to see whether Urdu will carry the day in this new extention and distinctly establish itself or end in evolving

The language question.

Of interest to linguistic student.

A new language. another variety of the horde or camp-bazaar language,—a curious 'pidgeon' amalgam or literary currency of Hindustani, Arabic, Turkish and other admixture of local patois and dialects. I am inclined, considering all the circumstances, to prognosticate the likelihood of the spread of Urdu *My own view.* as a spoken language in the regions of the three great rivers, thus enhancing its value and usefulness if not from its inherent strength and beauty then out of compliment to India for her sacrifices and services in opening out these ancient derelict lands to a new life of happy betterment, progress and prosperity. At the same time one may well look to some sort of bilingual *mélange* or *mésalliance* resulting from the extensive intercommunion of the Indian and Arab population in 'Mesopot' and round about that way. Again it is quite on the card, that this *The further spread of English.* extension of territory will undoubtedly lead to a wider spread and acceptance of the English language, a result by no means to be lightly regarded. The most widely-spoken of any language all over the entire world, the English language with its beautiful structure, its strength and sweetness of diction and its vast most magnificent and ever living literature must surely be made in the old as in the new Imperial possessions, as indeed it is, the one connecting and powerful chain to keep united all the various, far-flung parts and provinces that compose the Empire. Where flies the Union Jack there the general speech of all educated peoples must be the language spoken, written and illustrated by Shakespeare, Milton, Wordsworth, Burke, Byron, Longfellow, Emerson and a hundred other great and illustrious writers. In consolidating and organising *India's voice in Mesopotamia.* Mesopotamia as a component part of the Empire and in its future government India should claim to have and obtain if not a predominant yet a strong, leading and influential voice such as its vastly important position in and its superior services to the Empire, indisputably entitle it to. This is a conclusion of first significance and not to be overlooked or allowed to be neglected. It follows as a necessary corollary and in the very nature of things. For being nearest to India and in closest and readiest communication with it, Mesopotamia must be considered, as in fact it is, as of prime concern to this country, whether as regards commercial dealings, political importance, military value and needs, railway extensions to Westward, social and familiar intercourse and other cognate considerations.

Its value to India.

These observations and views may perhaps seem like skinning the bear and going shares in it before we have quite secured the bear. Not so; the observations are justified by events, for the bear is surely well within our grasp.

Views and observations not premature.

The capture and possession by our arms of practically all Mesopotamia, in spite of the shameful and cowardly Russian débacle, must be taken to be a *fait accompli*. If by any act of ours we lose hold of it, it will be our own fault and crass stupidity. But why should we be so previous as to assume that our rulers backed by our great Allies will, after fighting and worsting the Turk and the Boche in the way our armies have done and are doing, would be capable of such pusillanimity, inanition and invertebrate feebleness. In the very face of things any such supposition is not to be thought of unless you give up all ancient historical traditions of British valour, sound business instincts and tenacity of aim and purpose. We remain confident of a victorious peace; but merely supposing that things may not eventuate quite as we wish, the facts remain patent and convincing,—that the country is in cur hands, the inhabitants largely are willing to come under British Rule, their welfare and safety require it, great are and yet will be the sacrifices of Great Britain and India which call for compensation and all right and reason call for and persuade the extinction or deletion of Turkish misrule. Thus the only satisfying solution of the situation that has arisen where flow the Euphrates, the Tigris and the Shat' is annexation, and both good policy and expediency favour and support this eventuality.

CHAPTER LVII.

Return Voyage.

As the year was nearing its close, the good ship Zaiyanni turned her prow homewards. It was with regret I contemplated the finishing of my delightful holiday. At 7 a.m. on the 30th December 1916 we left Al Basra—Sinbad's City—the once famous seaport of the Caliphs and dropped down the river at half-speed. The regulations prescribe slackening speed all along the River, as the wash of the waters under anything like high-speed damages the shelving river banks. I kept my last lingering look on the ancient city till the great bend in the river where the Turkish ships are unavailingly sunk, hid it from view. I said good-bye to Basra, heartily wishing it a happy and prosperous future in British hands. At 9 a.m. we anchored abreast of Mohomerah. As the cargo we had to ship here for Bombay was not ready we missed the tide and had to lie up idly a whole twenty-four hours. Several B. I. steamers passed us quite close as we stood at anchor. In the afternoon a great South wind sprang up, and made the Zaiyanni drag her anchors, turn stern-end to the left-hand shore and get aground in the mud. At low tide the banks present a far stretch of fragrant mud. We had to put up steam and after some trouble righted the ship. Such a prank on the part of a big boat, wind and tide prevailing, during a dark night would create an awkward predicament. Ordinarily, however, large steamers after dark do not pass up or down this part of the Shat' where there is very little sea room, so that a collision which looks likely enough is very rare. All the same it is safest for a steamer to keep well to its proper berth: whilst here, a storm was brewing during the afternoon and burst in on us after midnight with great violence, much lightning and thunder and a heavy downpour of hail. Like all these

Gulf storms it lasted little over an hour. The morning rose bright, clear and crisp. Weighing anchor about 7 a.m. we passed Abadan town with its fine oil stench, and soon after desolate Fao. We cleared the Fao bar finely, but ran aground on the treacherous Basra bar. After some worry however the Captain got us off comfortably and all that day we were at sea in the Gulf with the rocky and bare Persian coast in view, the customary sea-gulls following us with untiring wing till sunset. On New Year's day at 1-30 a.m. We anchored safely in the inner Bushire harbour. The first thing my eye lighted on in the morning was the Kuh Khormaz with the sun cresting its pointed peak. The little gunboat Persepolis and the principal town-buildings ashore were all gaily dressed with multi-coloured bunting in honour of the New Year, 1917. Here we disembarked our large posse of the *Madzuris* whom we had taken on to Basra. Rough, uncouth, wild to look at, they turned out quite a cheery and peaceable lot, did their work and gave no trouble. Here too we dropped the Persian pilot. At 2 p.m. we started on our final run straight to Bombay. The old Persian town, seated amidst the blue waves, made a very presentable appearance in the bright afternoon. The last I saw of the land of Persia was the peak of Khormaz till it was dissolved in the dusk of the evening. The Zaiyanni, of which I shall always retain a pleasant recollection, doing her steady 10½ to eleven knots, brought us back to Bombay on the morning of the 7th January in something over six days from Bushire. A thick haze surrounded and shut off the Bombay coast and we had to pick our way in, stopping, easing, slowing and keeping a sharp lookout for the outstretching prongs. At 8 a.m. as the sun lifted the mist, we sighted the great outer lighthouse looming ghost-like in the distance. The pilot was aboard soon after and the Zaiyanni, just saving the tide, slipped inside the dockgates and was snugly warped up to her berth at 10-30 a.m., bringing us happily home again, after a delightful voyage of just one month, during which I visited and saw a world that was quite new to me and which I found exceedingly interesting and edifying.

FINIS